The Christ-Centered Woman

Finding Balance in a World of Extremes

Kimberly Dunnam Reisman

UPPER ROOM BOOKS®
NASHVILLE

THE CHRIST-CENTERED WOMAN

FINDING BALANCE IN A WORLD OF EXTREMES

Unless otherwise indicated, all scripture quotations are taken from the the New Revised Standard Version of the Bible,
copyright 1989, Division of Christian Education of the National Council of the Churches of Christ in the United
States of America. Used by permission. All rights reserved.

Scripture quotations identified as NLT are from the *Holy Bible*, New Living Translation, copyright © 1996.
Used by permission of Tyndale House Publishers, Inc., Wheaton, Illinois 60189. All rights reserved.

Scripture quotations identified as NIV are from the *Holy Bible, New International Version* copyright © 1973, 1978, 1984
International Bible Society. Used by permission of Zondervan Bible Publishers. All rights reserved.

Scripture quotations identified as JB are from *The Jerusalem Bible*, published and copyright © 1966, 1967, and 1968 by
Darton, Longman & Todd, Ltd., and Doubleday & Company, Inc. Used by permission of the publisher.

Scripture quotations identified as PHP are from *The New Testament in Modern English*
© 1958, 1960, 1972 by J. B. Phillips. Used by permission of The Macmillan Company.

Poem "Finding the We in Me" from *Dancing at My Funeral* by Maxie Dunnam.
Copyright © 1973 by Maxie Dunnam. Used by permission of the author.

Cover Design: Kirk DouPonce, David Uttley Design, Sisters, OR
Interior Design: Katherine Lloyd, David Uttley Design, Sisters, OR
Cover Photo: Superstock

Second printing: 2001
The Upper Room® Web site: http://www.upperroom.org

Library of Congress Cataloging-in-Publication Data
Reisman, Kimberly Dunnam, 1960-
      The Christ-centered woman : finding balance in a world of extremes / by Kimberly
Dunnam Reisman
        p. cm.
ISBN 0-8358-0913-7
      1. Christian women—Religious life. I. Title.

BV4527.R44 2000
        248.8'43—dc21   00-020067
                            Printed in the United States of America

The Christ-Centered Woman

To John,
my husband, friend, and playmate
on the merry-go-round of life.
Thank you for helping me keep my balance as it whirls
and for loving me even when the whirling flings me off.

CONTENTS

INTRODUCTION

The Call to Balance and Centeredness

atching my children grow up, I have always been amazed at the joy they've experienced on merry-go-rounds. These contraptions are no longer common on playgrounds today, probably due to the dangers they present, but my children loved them. The kids would hold on and push hard with their feet. As more children were attracted to the spinning and began pushing, the merry-go-round would turn faster and the children's laughter and squeals of delight would grow louder.

I watched this activity in awe that they could spin and spin without a hint of nausea, while I, simply observing, could hardly contain my churning stomach. But there they would be, hanging onto this whirling device, leaning way out, their heads flung back, hair flying, enjoying the speed. After awhile, they would tire of the effort required to hang on and scoot toward the center where the force of the turning was lessened.

As I began the inward exploration that always seems to launch my writing projects, I kept returning to these two contrasting images of the merry-go-round. The first was of my children holding on with all their might as the merry-go-round spun seemingly out of control. The second was of them moving to the center where the force decreased and their stability increased. Both images parallel the life experience of many of us.

The many and varied commitments of our lives often spin us at a dizzying rate. We live at such a pace that we feel we are either about to be flung off the whirling merry-go-round altogether, or we teeter dangerously close to losing our sense of balance. A friend whose husband was out of town on one of many business trips shared with me her sense of teetering. "Right now everything is under control," she said, "but a feeling of dread lurks in the back of my mind. What if one of the kids gets sick? What if the car breaks down?"

All of us, at one time or another, know the feeling of holding on with all our might while wishing for stability and balance. We need to find a center within, a place from which we can derive steadiness and equilibrium. As dizzy children move to the center of the merry-go-round where the force of spinning is less powerful, so we need to move to the center of ourselves where we can find strength and guidance to sort through the responsibilities that make up our lives. This book is a call to find that center. Through the process of inner contemplation, we have the potential to find for ourselves that restful part of the merry-go-round from which we can navigate the distracting forces of life.

The Search for Calm: My Story

A search for that center has been at the heart of my spiritual journey. Unlike many of my contemporaries, I have not followed a direct path. Many of the women I attended college with knew exactly where they were headed and went directly there. Law students, medical students, graduate students, they were motivated to achieve their goals and did just that. For me, however, the only constant and predictable element of my journey has been the need to explain the winding and circuitous path that has led to where I am now.

I have needed to "explain myself" in a variety of circumstances, but especially to the various ministry committees who examined me during my ordination process in the United Methodist Church, the hospital staff with whom I did a year-long residency in clinical pastoral education, and my seminary colleagues over the on-again, off-again pursuit of a graduate degree. The question I have always faced is, "Why has it taken you so long?"

I suppose it has taken me so long because, while I am not like many of my college friends who knew just what they wanted and went after it, I am like many other women. These women, from the beginning of their adulthood, felt pulled in many different directions. No one goal seemed to present itself. So they, and I, pursued several.

As I neared the end of my college years, I faced my first real exposure to the pressure of competing demands. I loved my major, English literature, and thought seriously about pursuing a doctorate in it. I also loved my other major, psychology, and was drawn to graduate work in that area as well. But neither sparked the passion within me necessary to dedicate untold hours of effort and substantial amounts of money to its pursuit. Neither enticed me the way my friends' careers enticed them.

Something, however, did spark my love and passion: my future husband, John. Unable to find my own niche, I chose to fit into his. He knew exactly where he was headed—medical school—and he wanted me with him on the journey. Had I given it deep thought at the time, I would have realized that two divergent forces were pulling at me. On one side was the lure of hearth and home; on the other, the tug of career and independence. As it was, I didn't feel conflicted at all. Rather I felt I was being quite pragmatic—committing myself to the one thing I was sure of, my love for John, while postponing a commitment to the things I was as yet unsure of.

My pragmatism worked for awhile. With a magnificent liberal arts education but precious little practical knowledge or experience, I entered the secretarial world to put food on the table while John was a full-time medical student. To this day I have the utmost respect for secretaries. I am confident that if my former bosses found out that I left the clerical arena, an incredible wave of thanksgiving would roll across the land. Needless to say, I quickly realized that I had to find something to be passionate about in addition to my marriage.

John fostered this realization as well. From the beginning he was clear about his expectation that I find for myself what he had found in medicine—

a sense of purpose, of calling, of personal fulfillment. His nightmare, he told me, was to have me awaken twenty years down the line and realize that in my desire to support and nurture him, I had failed to grow myself.

The Search for Self

I took John's words to heart and earnestly began to seek my own calling. Did I want to write? Did I want to counsel? We were still childless at that point, so I had the freedom to explore. A family friend, Buford Dickinson, was the president of a United Methodist seminary in our area. In his characteristically gentle way, Buford cajoled, urged, and challenged me about ministry. I didn't take him seriously at first, but later I decided that his idea might be worth exploring. I took an introductory course at the seminary. Soon after, Buford was diagnosed with cancer and died. His death and my relationship with his wife, Jean, throughout that experience brought my calling more sharply into focus. Jean made me aware of gifts that I had not yet discovered. Like Buford, she urged, challenged, and finally encouraged me to explore pastoral care. Because of her guidance I discovered a residency program in clinical pastoral education (CPE) that provided a stipend. I was accepted into the program and began my first steps toward ministry, determining finally that God was calling me to seminary.

Yet while I found myself newly committed to following God's call vocationally, my desire and passion for home and family life remained. Even as my excitement about ministry steadily grew, I was surprised to find myself thinking about children. Again, if I had explored these various feelings at any depth, I would have seen more clearly how they pushed and pulled against one another. And though I was somewhat aware of the fact that my desires might conflict, I assumed that I would be able to handle them both. Thus, about midway through my CPE residency program, I became pregnant with our first child.

As the ends of my residency program and my pregnancy drew near, the conflict became glaring. The CPE program ended in August, the baby was due in September, and John would graduate in June. Obviously I would not be able to start seminary right away, nor find any kind of work.

So again, I put my individual pursuits on hold. We took out a loan to live on for that last year of medical school, we had a beautiful baby boy, Nathan, and I immersed myself in new motherhood (with great joy, I might add).

That time was very special. Unlike previous periods of his training, John's last year of medical school was less stressful, and we saw him more. As he searched for surgical residency programs, I searched for seminaries. We decided that John would interview only at programs where a seminary existed within a commutable distance. We also decided that because he would finally be earning an income, I would be free to devote myself to graduate school.

After John graduated we moved and he began his surgical residency. I concentrated on settling us into our new home during the summer, but by the fall I had begun seminary. Because Nathan was only a year old, I chose to limit myself to studying three days a week. Looking back now, I wonder how we could have been so naïve. Surgical residencies are notoriously demanding, stressful, and exhausting. Why did I think I would have time for education? But our reasoning seemed sound at the time—I would need something to occupy myself beyond caring for Nathan during those long stretches of time alone.

I was definitely occupied and there were many long stretches of time alone. Yet we managed and I loved the seminary environment. Fortunately, Nathan enjoyed the family who cared for him while I was gone, which made my forty-minute morning commute more bearable. Once again, however, even as I was experiencing success in training for ministry, I longed for another child. And again, not recognizing the extent of the conflict inherent between these areas of responsibility, I became pregnant.

As my second year of seminary and my second pregnancy progressed, I learned a hard lesson about my ability to "handle it all": I couldn't. I knew I could be pregnant and work—I'd done that with Nathan. I knew I could go to school and care for my son—I'd done that too. But I discovered that on my own I couldn't go to school, care for Nathan, *and* be pregnant. My body wouldn't allow it. And my spirit struggled as well.

During the second semester I contracted pneumonia and withdrew from seminary. But after our daughter, Maggie, was born in April, I returned to school that fall and was able to continue uninterrupted. All told, I took only one extra year to get my degree. Still again, motherhood beckoned, and not surprisingly now that you know my pattern, I was pregnant with our third child when I graduated.

By the time of my graduation, I was on track to become a minister in the United Methodist Church. Under normal circumstances, after graduation I would have been ordained and received an appointment to a local church or other ministry. But by now, everyone knew that my circumstances were not "normal." John still had two years of training, we knew that we would probably not be staying in that part of the country, and I was pregnant to boot. Therefore, once again I settled down with my family to wait until a more opportune time to enter into active ministry. Our youngest, Hannah, was born the following December.

As John neared the end of his residency, he began looking for practices and I began looking again at ministry. When he joined a multispecialty clinic in Indiana, I was appointed to my first church. Because Nathan was just entering first grade, Maggie was four, and Hannah eighteen months, I accepted a quarter-time position as an associate pastor. I served at that church for four years. In 1997, feeling my children to be firmly in place in their appropriate schooling, I increased my workload to half time and was appointed as associate pastor at Trinity United Methodist Church where I currently serve.

The Saving Grace of a Calm Center

My long and winding journey would have been disastrous had I not discovered a calm center, nurtured over time, in my merry-go-round. There were many moments when I felt as though I would be flung off. Many times I frantically groped for the center in order to find stability and strength. Therefore I understand the need to feel balanced and centered, not because I have always achieved it, but because I know the difficulties encountered when I have not.

This book grew out of my own need to discover the place where I could find solace and guidance to sort through the responsibilities that I have sought and accepted. I know I am far from alone in this need; thus the creation of this book, in the hopes that through the process of inner contemplation, each of us can discover within the calm center from which to handle the distracting forces of life that can move us away from what is truly important.

There are many things that can make us stray from our center; some come from within, others are forced upon us. I will cover this in more depth in the following chapters. For now, however, I want to describe how a balanced woman acts so we know exactly what we're striving for.

First of all, the balanced woman, the person who has found her center, knows herself. She has established what is important to her and sets priorities and goals. Second, a Christ-centered woman is willing to make sacrifices for what she wants. Delayed gratification is a real and acceptable concept to her. Third, balanced women make wise judgments about how to achieve their goals; they seriously attempt to discern what to do and not do as they work toward their objectives. They are ready to make choices and commitments because they have tackled the task of ordering their souls.

It is usually easy to discern whether you have found your center. We are blessed when we find it and burdened when we do not. When we know where our center is, we have a sense of stability that allows us to negotiate the challenges of life with grace and perseverance. We are able to continue to ride the merry-go-round without falling off or tiring from the effort of holding on. When we are unbalanced, our lives exude chaos and frustration. We make impractical choices or none at all. We are easily upset by changes and new challenges. We cannot stick to any plan for long.

If you recognize yourself in the latter descriptions—and I have certainly been there—this book is for you. Be assured that a better method of coping is within your grasp.

Where Do We Start?

Here at the beginning it is important to note that achieving balance, developing a centered life, will not happen in the same way for each of us. Achieving balance will not even happen the same way over the course of a lifetime for any one person. At certain times favoring one area of our lives over another brings us balance, but that same favoring, at other times, may be what causes us to lose equilibrium. There is, however, a common denominator in our striving for Christ-centeredness. For all of us, at every point in our lives, it involves prayer for discernment and hard work to balance and order our souls.

Judging by the books I've encountered in my search for centeredness, in many ways we are approaching this need much the way the classical Greeks did. In their thinking, the root of evil was ignorance; therefore, the mind could surmount all problems. Reason, they said, is what saves us and temperance, or balance, is the rational ordering of our souls that comes through the exercise of our minds. Much of what we read today about balance encourages the exercise of the mind. If we organize ourselves, the experts suggest, make lists and stick to them, if we read enough self-help books and learn enough techniques, we will be able to balance all that life throws at us.

In contrast, the biblical notion of temperance or balance focuses not on the mind but on the heart. It is not the ignorance of our minds that is the root of evil but sin, the distortion of our hearts. Reason alone cannot save us; it can alleviate the problem of ignorance, but it cannot do anything about sin. Only Christ can do something about sin. Balance, therefore, does not occur because we exercise our minds and will it to happen. Balance occurs when we open ourselves to the power of the Holy Spirit to work in our hearts through our relationship with Jesus Christ. It is the living of a Spirit-filled, Christ-centered life.

And this is the starting point for our entire exploration: following Christ. I am a Christ-following woman. Jesus is the means through which God becomes real for me as well as for other Christ followers. When we look at Jesus, we can see who God is and what God is like, and it is through our relationship with Jesus that we are able to gain an understanding of our truest selves and find the source of our centeredness.

You may not be a Christ follower, yet you may still be on a quest for balance and centeredness. You may have a relationship with Christ but not yet made that relationship an integral part of your interior life. You may have been a Christ follower for a long time who is looking for continued depth in the journey. Wherever you are on life's road, even if those travels have until now not involved Christ, I hope that as you read this book you will open yourself to the possibility that God is reaching out to you through Jesus, that God desires wholeness and balance for your life, and that centeredness can be found in Christ.

A Difficult Journey, But Not a Lonely One

No matter who you are, this journey is not an easy one. Society holds out many avenues toward centeredness. Many of them focus on self as healer, teacher, and guide. Many of us wander unaided and unguided, searching within ourselves for the center that will provide us with lasting stability and equilibrium.

As Christ followers, we are fortunate that our quest is not unaided. It may be an inward journey, but it is not an isolated one. We do not have to search high and low for a source of our centeredness; we have been given a center for our lives. Paul wrote, "I pray that from his glorious, unlimited resources he [God] will give you mighty inner strength through his Holy Spirit. And I pray that Christ will be more and more at home in your hearts as you trust in him" (Eph. 3:16-17, NLT). Christ is our center. He is the one to whom we look to provide order for our souls. He guards us against imbalance. "When Christ is the Lord of our lives, nothing else can be; when Christ is not Lord of our lives, anything and everything else will be."[1]

Christ at the center places all our demands and obligations, all our responsibilities and commitments, all our hopes and desires into perspective. When our lives are focused on Christ, we become open to the Holy Spirit's power to keep us balanced. We are able to recognize that balance is not a matter of following special rules or mastering a particular technique, but a matter of discovering our truest self, the whole self God created us to be. When Christ is our center, we are empowered to make decisions based on what is right for that *true self*, not necessarily what is right for anyone else. This kind of centeredness allows us to lead more relaxed, ordered lives and move confidently toward the abundant life that God intended for us.

Jesus has invited us to learn this kind of balance. Jesus said, "Come to me, all you that are weary and are carrying heavy burdens, and I will give you rest. Take my yoke upon you, and learn from me; for I am gentle and humble in heart, and you will find rest for your souls. For my yoke is easy, and my burden is light" (Matt. 11:28-30).

How, then, do we find this rest? To begin, we need to discover a new framework on which to build our lives. Let me introduce a new metaphor: I find the picture of a wheel helpful. If Christ is to be the center, we need strong, reliable spokes leading to the wheel surface that actually hits the road of our lives. The unbalance and chaos we have experienced reveal that we have been relying upon uncertain spokes. In the chapters that follow, I am going to share new spokes with you—biblical tools for realizing Christ-centeredness as a lifestyle.

Friend, be encouraged. Though this is a difficult journey, it is one God aids and blesses. You see, God is not "put off" by our imperfection in this area. God does not wait for us to have our spiritual acts together before reaching out to us and seeking relationship with us. This should be a point of great relief and freedom for us, for while we may strive for a sense of centeredness and balance, our relationship with God is not dependent upon our success. God's love will remain steadfast regardless. This is a great motivator for us as well, for as we become less focused on our own abilities, performance, skill, or mastery, we will become more and more focused on Christ and Christ's leading in our lives.

With Christ as our center, the merry-go-round will not fling us off. The wheel we ride upon on our life journey will provide a steady ride, despite speed bumps, potholes, and detours. We can stand firm, balanced and centered and ready to face the challenges of our lives.

Part One

Coping with Obstacles to Christ-Centeredness

ONE

🦢

The Bondage of Stereotypes:
Susie Homemaker and Superwoman

s we journey toward centeredness and the wholeness it can bring, we never all begin at the same place. As I mentioned in the Introduction, some of us may be searching for our center but have yet to entertain the notion that our center might be in Jesus Christ. Others may have a relationship with Christ but not yet made that relationship an integral part of their interior lives. Still others may have been following Christ for a long time and are looking for continued depth for their journey. Perhaps many of us are somewhere in-between.

Regardless of where we begin our journey, however, each of us is bound to encounter obstacles to achieving centeredness. It is the nature of the spiritual process. These blocks can come both from within ourselves and from without; and while the details of our stories may be different, many of the obstacles are common to us all.

I want to begin our journey together by focusing on some of the outer means that hinder us from moving toward a sense of centeredness. These are ways in which our culture, specifically American culture, works overtly and covertly to move us away from our center and toward the distraction of the superficial. While this is not a how-to-get-organized book, a great deal of what distracts us has to do with our responsibilities in the world and the expectations that world has for us. Because of this, it is impossible to work toward Christ-centeredness without spending at least some time discussing the issues of ordinary life—motherhood, careers, vocations, household responsibilities, and societal expectations.

I want to begin by focusing on two specific myths that secular and religious culture offer us, which, if believed, hinder us from placing Christ at the center of our lives. I call these the myths of Susie Homemaker (you remember little Susie playing with her Easy-Bake Oven, don't you?) and Superwoman. You will probably recognize these amazing women quickly.

Myth 1: Susie Homemaker

Professor, writer, and lecturer Mary Ellen Ashcroft often begins her workshops by asking the participants to make a list of at least twenty attributes of a "really good" woman. She has performed this experiment in dramatically different settings, from small, radical liberal arts colleges to gatherings of conservative Baptist women, and with women of all ages, denominations, and backgrounds. Over the years she has compiled a surprisingly homogenous description of this "really good" woman. This woman seems to live all over the country, is a member of almost every church, knows no economic boundary, and inhabits both the countryside and our cities. We all seem to know and love her. Who is she? I will let Ashcroft introduce her to you:

> Her children are clean and neatly dressed.
> . . . She bakes for her kids' lunches and for after-school snacks. The smell of dinner is usually wafting around an hour or so before hubby comes in. Often concerned that there might not be enough, she cooks more than she needs to. After everyone is seated, she keeps scurrying around, making sure everyone has what they need.
> She's the one who is usually waiting to pick up the kids in the van after school. But if she's not the chauffeur, she prefers to ride in the back.

. . . She keeps up on the family correspondence. She writes to her husband's family as well as her own, and is in charge of inviting people over for dinner.

She worries quite a lot about her weight. It would be bad if she put on too much and became unattractive to her husband. She exercises a bit to keep her weight down.

She hates to keep people waiting. For her the feeling of causing even the smallest inconvenience for someone is very hard. She apologizes a lot, as if even her existence is a nuisance. "I'm sorry," she says. "Excuse me." "I seem to be in the way." "Can you see okay?"

. . . She is very sweet. She tries not to lose her temper. Just under the sweet exterior is an air of anxiety, of distraction. Where did I put that recipe? Where should I buy the pork chops? What if Joey has forgotten his homework? Should I serve the salad before the main course or with it?[1]

I have met this woman. Haven't you? You might think that the uniformity of our perceptions and the command they have over us developed because biblical teaching or another highly regarded authority created this perfect woman. Certainly it would make more sense. Strangely enough, this isn't the case. Susie arrived on the scene not in biblical times, but in the Victorian era, and she's been with us ever since. Television, movies, books, magazines, cartoons, and commercials have over the years enhanced Susie's perfection and solidified her power over us.

Where Susie Came From

We can get a better understanding of the Susie Homemaker myth and its power if we look at how society generally viewed men, women, and work before she was born. Prior to the industrial revolution, the focus of work for both men and women was the household. This was where things were made and used. Work was hard for everyone; there was always a lot of it, and men and women worked side by side to get it done. The

Protestant traditions particularly supported the idea that each person's hard work was a virtue and was intimately connected with salvation. Our term, "the Protestant work ethic," originated from this outlook.

Over decades, however, things began to change. Separate spheres of work began to replace shared work. The industrial revolution of the nineteenth century is the most obvious marker in this process of change. Starting in Britain, it not only created gigantic advances in technology, it led to immense changes in lifestyle, not the least of which was the birth of the middle class. In a culture that had always been characterized by a rigid class separation, societal anxiety began to arise as money and possessions blurred the distinctions between business owners and the aristocracy.

According to historians, the anxiety caused by class mobility as well as other factors is central to understanding Victorian culture. Anxiety highlights the Victorian response, which was to search for secure footing in the face of rapid change. The rock on which British (and later American) society began to stand for security was the home.[2]

Home as a focus was not a new idea in and of itself. The home had long been the center of life, the place where you slept and ate and worked and lived. The Victorian age brought the notion that the home was a refuge amidst the storms of life, and one person in particular belonged there—the wife.

Susie Homemaker had arrived, and with her came the creation of separate spheres of life and a new sense of "otherness"—the idea of the opposite sex. Like Susie Homemaker herself, the idea of men and women being opposites has been with us for so long we often mistakenly believe it's biblical. Actually it's another Victorian concept that has a stranglehold on our consciousness.

With the rise of the home as a haven came the rise of the idea of the sexes as polar opposites, each existing in a completely separate domain. The male realm was the dog-eat-dog world of work. Being tough and competitive, aggressive and "self-made" enabled our men to fight for a living for their families. They became known during this time as "breadwinners."

Wives began to be referred to as "dependents" and female workers were no longer called "ladies" but "girls."[3]

According to this thinking, the home front was naturally an opposite type of environment from the working world, a place of peace and refuge from the rat race that raged outside. The perfect woman was opposite as well. Where her husband was assertive and determined, she was motherly and self-sacrificing. Where he was lusty and macho, she was pure.

Mars and Venus in the Victorian Era

A writer of the Victorian era, John Ruskin, was instrumental in solidifying the notion of polar opposites. His essay, "Of Queens' Garden," had a dramatic effect on Victorian thinking about men and women: "Each has what the other has not: each completes the other, and is completed by the other: they are in nothing alike."[4] What a far cry from Adam's joyful response to Eve: "This at last is bone of my bones and flesh of my flesh" (Gen. 2:23)! Yet Ruskin's idea of separate and opposite spheres of function took hold and shaped our image of Susie Homemaker.

According to Ruskin, Susie may be gentle and motherly, but she is also instrumental in influencing men. He placed the responsibility of raising morally superior children squarely on her shoulders because she herself was morally superior: "So far as she rules, all must be right, or nothing is. She must be enduringly, incorruptibly good; instinctively, infallibly wise—wise, not for self-development, but for self-renunciation."[5]

Is it any wonder guilt has plagued women over every choice and decision they make? Is it any wonder that we often feel responsible for everything within our realm of experience?

While it feels as though Susie Homemaker was created alongside Eve in the garden, it helps us to recognize that she actually arose in Britain from the Victorian belief that God had authored a codependency between the sexes. We gain strength through the realization that God is not at the heart of this myth; Victorian thinking is. And note: Susie may have originated in Britain, but she was not limited by geography. She quickly departed for America, where she took hold of our collective consciousness as well.

THE WRATH OF SUSIE

Now that we understand her creation, it's also important to understand Susie's impact on society. Both men and women suffered from her stature as a middle-class ideal. For example, a woman's status as a "lady" depended upon not working. Men became pressured to work longer hours to solely provide for their families, causing them to see their families less. Unmarried women in particular had a raw deal. If they missed out on marriage, they couldn't even take up meaningful work without sacrificing their image as "good women." Hence we have the "spinster's" marginalized role in society and a child's card game named in her honor—Old Maid.

In reality, few women beyond the upper classes could achieve the Susie Homemaker epitome of womanhood. Living on a single income was a distant dream for most families in the late nineteenth and early twentieth centuries. The poor in particular were excluded from the ideal, but as in our own time, few voices were raised in defense of those who were too poor not to work.

Despite this reality, the myth of Susie Homemaker kept its hold as the standard women ought to reflect, particularly in the mid-twentieth century and in the West.

The traditional family, which originated in the fifties and sixties and was led at home by Susie Homemaker and in the work force by her husband, took its toll on women. As astounding as it may seem now, society viewed women as unable to comprehend—or at least to be completely disinterested in—the arena of the mind, of intellect and ideas, of soul and spirit. Comments made at a meeting of magazine editors during those years depicts this demeaning side effect of Susie's presence in our culture.

Our readers are housewives, full time. They're not interested in the broad public issues of the day. They are not interested in national or international affairs. . . . They aren't interested in politics, unless it's related to an immediate need in the home, like the price of coffee. Humor? Has to be gentle, they don't get satire. Travel? We have almost completely dropped it. . . . You just can't write about ideas or broad issues of the day for women. That's why we're publishing 90 percent service now and 10 percent general interest.[6]

THE TRUTH ABOUT SUSIE

We shouldn't be surprised then at the stir Betty Friedan caused when she wrote *The Feminine Mystique* in 1963. Researching, interviewing, and writing for five years, Friedan simply wanted to answer the question: Why are women so unhappy when they supposedly have it all? According to the media, happy housewives abounded in America; women everywhere were content to stay at home, tending the house and children while their men were away at work. Yet rather than finding even one happy housewife, Friedan found women suffering from everything from simple boredom to depression. She witnessed a "nameless aching dissatisfaction" that drove record numbers of women to tranquilizer use as well as drug and alcohol abuse. One woman told Friedan, "You wake up in the morning, and you feel as if there's no point in going on another day like this. So you take a tranquilizer because it makes you not care so much that it's pointless."[7]

In the time leading up to the release of her book, Friedan determined that the "mystique" of the feminine, that "otherness" created so carefully in the Victorian era, "permits, even encourages, women to ignore the question of their identity. The mystique says that they can answer the question 'Who am I?' by saying 'Tom's wife . . . Mary's mother.' . . . The truth is . . . an American woman no longer has a private image to tell her who she is, or can be, or wants to be."[8]

This mystique, this image of Susie Homemaker and its power over women, cost them personal growth. It cost them the opportunity to explore their interior selves—their minds—their spirits. Annie Roiphe, in her book *Fruitful*, confirms this: "Now we can talk about self-fulfillment, career or profession, now we can have ambitions, disappointments, economic responsibility, lust, love. Then we had only vicarious accomplishments, vicarious triumphs and failures. We had limits on our growth, limits on our potential, limits everywhere."[9]

Those limits extended even to Christian service. So ingrained was Susie Homemaker in our religious consciousness that even today we often believe that to be like her is the God-given calling of all women. What has actually happened is that Christians have swallowed—hook, line, and sinker—the Victorian cultural artifact of Susie Homemaker and accepted her image as gospel truth when in fact secular culture created this image, not biblical teaching. The call of Jesus—to follow and become disciples—was the same to both men and women. Women were an integral part of Jesus' ministry, and scripture seems to paint a picture of the early church as one where gifts and callings took precedence over gender. Yet Susie's myth was pervasive enough to infiltrate church teaching and create a tradition where women regularly confront gender prejudice regarding their abilities. We are still fighting this myth in many churches (though thankfully, not in mine).

As a woman who came of age in the eighties, I haven't experienced the extent of the limits Susie Homemaker placed on Roiphe, Friedan, and their peers during those years. The astonishment and offense I feel when I read books like Friedan's is a testament to how far we have come in separating ourselves from Susie's image.

A phone conversation with my mother drove that accomplishment home to me recently. She called to share her excitement over being asked to speak (preach, although she didn't use that word) in the weekly chapel service at the seminary where my father is president. She was thrilled and proud and I was very happy for her, yet at the same time I found myself somewhat saddened by her joy. It was as though she was surprised that they would ask her, as though it was a unique and unusual thing for her to be asked to speak in such a significant environment.

I took for granted that my mother would have something meaningful and valuable to share with those at the seminary. I found it natural that people would want to hear her speak, not only because of her vast experience in ministries of all kinds, but because of the way in which she is gifted to communicate. Yet she did not seem to find this natural at all.

The contrast between my mother's reaction and mine indicates that Susie has lost much of her power. Clearly, as we have discovered that Susie isn't as remarkably balanced and happy as we thought, she has begun to lose her hold on us. Many have even realized that in real life, she never truly existed at all.

We no longer consciously feel the limits she once placed on us. Yet Susie's image lingers in the backgrounds of our psyches, layered with the memories of playing with our Easy-Bake Ovens. When I feel solely responsible for my children's problems, I can sense her out there. When I feel guilty for not having a spotless house or for "letting" my husband cook dinner (he likes to do it more than I do anyway), I know she's lurking in the corner of my mind. Fortunately, because of a lot of history and a decent amount of social upheaval, I now understand that Susie is a myth that blocks my way toward a centered life. Yet that knowledge too has come with a price, the price of another myth.

Myth 2: Superwoman

While society continues to have strong messages for women about what they can and cannot do, we have more choices today than ever before. For this we can thank the Women's Movement. As conflicted as we may feel about the movement's current status, few of us would want to backtrack. Most of us take for granted that we can vote, that we can offer evidence in a court of law, that we have recourses for sexual harassment, or that we won't be denied a higher education because of our gender. Whatever our political stance at the dawn of the twenty-first century, we owe a debt of gratitude to the courageous women who went before us.

As much as we have gained over the years, we must also admit that our lives are much more complicated as a result of the many choices we have available to us. Along with that complexity came a new untouchable role model: Superwoman. Where my mother's generation had to contend with Susie Homemaker, this is the myth that haunts my generation. As with Susie, we strengthen our understanding of Superwoman, and thus our ability to confront her, when we look at the history that led to her creation.

While I am not a social scientist, the myth of Superwoman appears to me to be a backlash against a backlash. First was the feminist rejection of the constraints of Susie Homemaker: as the fifties faded into the sixties and women heard the distant rumblings of the feminist movement, a great sigh of relief went up all over the country: *I am a person—with hopes and disappointments and passions and abilities. And I am ready to express them all.*

As exciting as this new concept appeared, as true as it felt to women everywhere, it quickly ran head-on into the reality of motherhood. The dawn of the seventies saw *home* and *family* become dirty words. Motherhood was viewed as capitulation to an Old World order. In this environment, many women rejected the roles of the past and headed off to the workplace. They entered the male-dominated world of work in droves and many excelled. Women began to move up the corporate ladder and for the first time experienced financial success independent of men. Yet more and more, women were placed between a rock and a hard place. Motherhood and the call of the "traditional life" were diametrically opposed to the feminist commitment. The very nature of motherhood is the activity of caring for another, placing the needs of that other ahead of your own. Feminism, in dramatic contrast, insisted on "attention being paid to the self, to the full humanity, wishes, desires, capacities of the self."[10]

Despite this conflict, women continued to get married and have babies. The shrill rejection of men and children didn't completely ring true in the everyday life of women outside the university walls. If the feminist movement was a backlash against the power of Susie Homemaker, then the myth of Superwoman was a backlash against the all-or-nothing attitude of the feminist movement. Women in my generation absorbed the feminist message that they were capable and independent and able to pursue any career they chose. We agreed with the need for equal pay for equal work. But most of us still wanted to marry and to have children. We didn't want to give up everything to pursue a career—we wanted it all. And precisely because of the feminist message of independence, we were confident that we could have it.

Superwoman arrived to save us all from the burden of choice. We could be Susie Homemaker and a Liberated Woman at the same time! The American media quickly latched on to this new myth. Women's magazines expanded their offerings to include guidelines for choosing the right day care, tips to help organize chaotic mornings when the whole family was trying to get off to school and work, fashion sections emphasizing wardrobes that could take you from home to work to evening, and articles on the value of "quality" time—as opposed to quantity of time—spent with children.

Women (with a surprising amount of support from men) have embraced the myth of Superwoman and have launched into exciting careers while continuing to hold down the fort at home. But again, this has not been without price. While a danger of the Susie Homemaker myth is that it limits women to only one outlet for self-expression, a danger of the Superwoman myth is that it assumes unlimited energy and resources in pursuing self-expression, personal growth, and fulfillment. The reality is quite the opposite. Actress Meg Ryan stated the situation succinctly in a comment to her business partner, "Being a working mother means that you are always disappointing somebody."[11]

The truth is, our resources are never unlimited. While there are men who share with their wives the burden of juggling home life with a career, the more common reality is that Superwoman finds herself single-handedly working two full-time jobs—when her shift at her paying job ends, her shift at home begins. We can't be all things to all people. Somewhere along the line someone is going to get the short end of the stick; it may be us, it may be our families, or it may be our work. Meg Ryan was right: someone is going to be disappointed.

We shouldn't make the mistake of thinking that the pressure to be a Superwoman is limited to married women with children. Unlike Susie Homemaker, Superwoman is truly inclusive. Unmarried women have often experienced their career climb to be a soul-draining experience that consumes precious time and blocks opportunities to develop healthy relationships. Single mothers know too well the limits that a twenty-four-

hour day can bring. And of course, poor women have always been struggling to be Superwomen, quietly juggling jobs and home for lack of any
other choice.

If Susie Homemaker is dangerous because of her limitations,
Superwoman is dangerous because of her expansiveness. No one can do it
all, at least not at the same time, and not always successfully or long term.
I learned this firsthand during seminary when I became pregnant with my
second child, Maggie. Thoroughly swayed by the Superwoman myth, I
had evidence that I could do it all. I'd been pregnant and worked before.
I'd been in school with a small child before. But I had never gone to
school, cared for a small child, and been pregnant at the same time. The
reality was that my body wouldn't allow me to do it all.

As I mentioned in the Introduction, I ultimately contracted pneumonia and withdrew from seminary. Yet when I buckled under the strain
of trying to be a bona fide Superwoman, rather than questioning the
validity of the myth, I questioned myself. I believe many women do.
Rather than recognizing the mistake of trying to do it all, we doubt our
own abilities. Why can't we handle it? Other women don't seem to be
having any trouble. Why aren't we stronger? Why don't we have more
energy? The secret that Superwoman hides is that no one can really be
one. Just like Susie Homemaker, Superwoman exists only in our minds.
But our minds can really deceive us!

We live in an age of unprecedented workaholism and burnout.
Businesses continue to downsize, leaving fewer people to do more work.
Superwoman was tailor-made for these conditions because she lulls us into
thinking that we can do it, and that everyone else already is doing it. She
convinces us that there are no boundaries. She entices us with the belief
that everything is possible if we just work hard enough. But living with the
Superwoman myth is living in a dream world—a nightmare, actually. In
that world we are destined not only for exhaustion but fragmentation. We
will never be able to move toward wholeness if we fail to set boundaries
for ourselves. We cannot experience the centeredness that God intends
for us if we falsely believe we can do it all.

Moving beyond the Myths

The problem with each of the myths we've looked at is that they are impractical ideals, wrapped up too neatly to exist in the real world. Our lives are bigger, fuller, and packed with more potential meaning than any of these myths can handle. Blindly accepting them without regard for what is valuable and what needs to be jettisoned derails us from our journey toward centeredness.

While the myths we've discussed are harmful if believed in their entirety, it's important to recognize that each contains a grain of truth for our journey toward balance and centeredness. Saying no to Susie Homemaker does not mean that we abandon our homes or our families. Rejecting Superwoman does not mean that we relinquish our desire to pursue more than one avenue with our talents. Rather we must find a better way to live our lives than these stereotypes allow. We must find a way to move beyond the myths to the centeredness that Christ offers us.

How do we do that? For me, the story of Ruth has provided a very helpful tool. Many of us know the story, but my focus will probably surprise you. Let's read the story again.

> In the days when the judges ruled, there was a famine in the land, and a certain man of Bethlehem in Judah went to live in the country of Moab, he and his wife and two sons. The name of the man was Elimelech and the name of his wife Naomi, and the names of his two sons were Mahlon and Chilion. . . . They went into the country of Moab and remained there. But Elimelech, husband of Naomi, died, and she was left with her two sons. These took Moabite wives; the name of the one was Orpah and the name of the other Ruth. When they had lived there about ten years, both Mahlon and Chilion also died, so that the woman was left without her two sons and her husband.
>
> Then she started to return with her daughters-in-law from the country of Moab, for she had heard in the country of Moab that the LORD had considered his people and given them food. So she

set out from the place where she had been living, she and her two daughters-in-law, and they went on their way to go back to the land of Judah. But Naomi said to her two daughters-in-law, "Go back each of you to your mother's house. May the LORD deal kindly with you, as you have dealt with the dead and with me. The LORD grant that you may find security, each of you in the house of your husband." Then she kissed them, and they wept aloud. They said to her, "No, we will return with you to your people." But Naomi said, "Turn back, my daughters, why will you go with me? Do I still have sons in my womb that they may become your husbands? Turn back, my daughters, go your way, for I am too old to have a husband. Even if I thought there was hope for me, even if I should have a husband tonight and bear sons, would you then wait until they were grown? Would you then refrain from marrying? No, my daughters, it has been far more bitter for me than for you, because the hand of the LORD has turned against me." Then they wept aloud again. Orpah kissed her mother-in-law, but Ruth clung to her.

So she said, "See, your sister-in-law has gone back to her people and to her gods; return after your sister-in-law." But Ruth said,

"Do not press me to leave you
    or to turn back from following you!
Where you go, I will go;
    where you lodge, I will lodge;
your people shall be my people,
    and your God my God.
Where you die, I will die—there will I be buried.
    May the Lord do thus and so to me, and more as well,
if even death parts me from you!"

When Naomi saw that she was determined to go with her, she said no more to her.

So the two of them went on until they came to Bethlehem.

(Ruth 1:1-19)

What a wonderful story of love and commitment! Over the years we have lifted up Ruth as the hero of this story, and rightly so. Her courage and loyalty are admirable and her decision to follow Naomi was crucial to the continuation of the line of David, which eventually led to Jesus.

Orpah, on the other hand, is the mystery character in the drama. As quickly as she entered the picture, she left it. After she returned to her family we heard nothing more about her. But her presence was important. It made the story richer and deeper, which is why it has come to hold such meaning for me.

As you can probably guess, women in Naomi, Ruth, and Orpah's time were in a precarious position. They depended upon men for their security and well-being. Widows were particularly vulnerable. They had virtually no rights. No one was obligated to care for them. If a widow were fortunate, her family would take her in after her husband died and provide for her. If she had no family, however, she was cast out of society and left to fend for herself. That was quite a frightening prospect then as now.

When Naomi was widowed, she remained secure even though she was in a foreign land because her sons were able to care for her. When the sons died, however, all three women were placed in a difficult situation. Naturally, Naomi decided to return to Bethlehem. There was no one in Moab to care for her; the famine in her homeland was over; it was a wise decision to return to the protected environment of her family. The same reasoning that compelled Naomi to return home led her to urge Ruth and Orpah to return to their families as well. If they went with her, there was no guarantee that they would be accepted. Instead they would become the foreigners, widowed and alone, and their well-being was not assured.

It's important to remember that neither woman wanted to leave Naomi. Both Ruth and Orpah had such love for their mother-in-law that they wanted to stay with her. All three had already started the journey to Judah—the conversation that we witness occurred on the way. It was a heart-wrenching scene: they were sobbing and clinging to each other. The decision was not made easily. They talked and cried and talked and cried.

Finally Orpah decided to leave. In the midst of the weeping she kissed Naomi good-bye and departed.

It was after Orpah left that Ruth so beautifully expressed her commitment to Naomi: "Where you go, I will go; where you lodge, I will lodge; your people shall be my people, and your God my God" (Ruth 1:16). Ruth made the courageous choice to leave the safety of her homeland and journey to a foreign one. It was a wonderful testament to loyalty and love, and Naomi quickly realized that Ruth would not be deterred.

And the Hero Is . . .

I have always admired Ruth and her courage. I frequently look to her for inspiration when I have difficult decisions to make. Yet I believe we can learn from Orpah as well—that seemingly insignificant character who disappeared, never to be heard from again. I believe that Orpah made a good and a right decision. As admirable as Ruth's choice was, Orpah's decision was based on solid reasoning. In light of the lack of status and security widows experienced in those times, it made sense for Orpah to return to the security of the only family she had. It was a tremendous risk to go to Bethlehem as a foreigner with no guarantee that Naomi's family would care for her.

Orpah made a wise decision, but Orpah did not follow. Ruth followed; she followed Naomi. There is obvious tension between these two choices. There was no middle option. Our lives often feel the same way. We often feel that between two opposing choices, only one of them is right. Society and the church often encourage us to think that way. Just as our culture would have us believe various myths, it also would have us believe that there is only one "right" decision among many. All too often, the church, either directly or indirectly, supports this position. Ruth made the "right" choice; Orpah made the "wrong" one. If you don't choose to be Ruth, the message from all the Ruths out there is that you are completely misguided. If you don't choose to be Orpah, the message from all the Orpahs out there is exactly the same.

I do not believe that God intended our lives to be made up of such extremes. The value we gain from the story of Ruth and Orpah is not that

Ruth made the right choice and Orpah did not, but that both women made choices that were right for them individually. We don't hear from Orpah again, but we can probably assume that after she returned home, she led a secure life. We know that Ruth went on to be an integral part of our salvation story. Both women made right choices, choices that were *good enough* for their individual circumstances and the plan of God for their lives.

The Spoke of "Good Enough"

The words *good enough* are key as we seek to find a sense of centeredness for ourselves and to live according to God's plan for our lives. We live in a world of conflicting demands and seemingly limitless choices. All those choices, even the small ones, are intertwined with our faith. Our faith will determine what we value and what types of commitments we will be willing to make. These commitments then affect the growth of our faith. The necessity of making choices in a world of competing demands emphasizes our need to understand the concept of "good enough." It is a vital spoke for our wheel.

One of the valuable cultural messages we receive is the importance of pursuing excellence. Whether it is in the world of sports, education, or the workplace, society rewards excellence. Scripture strengthens this message as well. Paul wrote to the church at Philippi, "If there is any excellence and if there is anything worthy of praise, think about these things" (Phil. 4:8). Excellence is a noble aspiration. I believe it pleases God when we strive to be the best we can be, using the gifts God placed within us to their fullest potential. Just as the idea of excellence can be motivating, however, it can be damaging as well. Many families have suffered the pain of being ignored by a workaholic striving to be the best employee. Many women have damaged their bodies and their spirits attempting to attain an ideal, "excellent" body shape. Both men and women have approached the point of sheer exhaustion trying to be all things to all people. As valuable as the notion of excellence is, there is a desperate need for the notion of "good enough" as well.

I confronted my own need for such a concept during seminary. When I began, I was extremely stressed and had great difficulty finding the rhythm of academics that I had so often experienced in the past. During my college years, I was used to hard work and excellent grades, so I instinctively reverted to those study habits and expectations. Unfortunately, the academic pattern didn't fall together the way it had for me in college. What I overlooked was the fact that the current circumstances of my life in no way resembled those of my college years. I was married; I had an infant; and John was in the midst of a time-consuming surgical residency.

As I struggled to juggle the demands of home and school, I quickly realized that I couldn't give adequate time and energy to both school and my son. That also meant I couldn't be the "ideal" mother or student of my dreams. The challenge I faced was to find balance, a way to be a "good enough" seminary student and a "good enough" mother. Even more challenging was accepting that excellence was not necessary at this point, simply being "good enough" at both of those aspects of my life was. (The irony of discovering the notion of "good enough" was that once I recognized it, I found the rhythm that had been missing and began to excel once more at school while maintaining a happy life at home as well.)

I still expect excellence of myself in most pursuits. I'm thankful that my family continually reinforces the importance of "good enough" for me. I recall a Mother's Day card my middle daughter, Maggie, made me a few years ago. On the inside she wrote, "My mother knows about God and cooking." She didn't say I knew all there was to know about God or cooking, but I obviously know enough about both to satisfy her need for spiritual nurture and good health. And that is good enough for me.

Orpah and Us

Orpah understood "good enough." She made a very difficult decision, one filled with the pain of separation and loss, but one that was good enough for her. As we look for a new framework on which to build the structure of our lives, a first step is to claim that for ourselves. The concept of "good enough" can provide a strong spoke for the wheel of our life, a spoke that leads from Christ at the center outward toward the many decisions and choices we face every day.

This notion has countless applications. We all need to make choices that help us become "good enough" mothers, children, siblings, workers, volunteers, and friends. The "good enough" spoke moves us one step away from the Superwoman and Susie Homemaker myths that would confine and confuse us and one step closer to our center and to wholeness. It enables us to look at the choices that lay before us not from the world's perspective of what is appropriate, but from our own insights about what is right for us. Orpah showed us the way.

Two

2

The Calling of Many Voices: Fragmentation

e have discussed some of the external challenges to finding a sense of balance in our lives; now we turn to an internal challenge. The word *fragmentation* suggests its definition: the splitting of a whole into many pieces or fragments. Fragmentation, then, challenges us in two specific ways. The first is when we allow one part of ourselves to dominate the other parts. You see this in a person who is an obsessive shopper, for example. The second is the tendency to become compartmentalized or separated into many different parts. When we are fragmented we feel pulled apart by all the things that compete for our attention. You see this in a person who continually overcommits herself. Both of these types of fragmentation hinder us from being the whole, integrated selves God desires us to be.

Type 1: When One Part Rules

The easiest way to understand the first type of fragmentation, which occurs when a part of ourselves dominates our entire being, is to look at addiction. When we become addicted to something, our craving for the substance takes over and our lives begin to revolve around it. Alcoholism and drug abuse are two obvious examples of a part dominating the whole.

But drug addicts and alcoholics aren't the only ones who suffer from this kind of fragmentation; anyone can.

Any time an element of our lives becomes forceful enough to push out other concerns and divert our attention, we run the risk of becoming fragmented. If we are so focused on our job, for example, that we fail to recognize the needs of those around us, or even the wider variety of our own needs, we are traveling the road to a divided self. If we become so engrossed in the everyday goings-on of our children or other family members that we miss opportunities for personal growth and challenge, our path to centeredness is blocked.

Certainly there are times in each of our lives when a part of us must dominate the whole. When we are facing serious illness, either our own or that of a family member, it is natural to devote our energies to that situation. When we are grieving the loss of a loved one through death or divorce, it is normal to concentrate for a time on the bereavement. In these cases, fragmentation actually works in our favor, allowing our temporary focus on pressing needs. Less calamitous but equally diverting are the times when we must tackle important projects that are beneficial to our overall personal growth, or simply required by our jobs or volunteer commitments.

What we must guard against are not the isolated incidents that motivate domination by a single part of ourselves, but the patterns that can develop. If we are not deliberate about finding a center for ourselves, and making "good enough" decisions based on that foundation, it is easy to find ourselves suddenly consumed by one particular aspect of our lives. When we encounter a challenge to our stability like illness or grief, if we do not work to grow and heal in the midst of that circumstance, we can develop of pattern of self-pity or inertia. Such patterns can take hold and then the temporary fragmentation that is bound to occur now and again becomes an unhealthy aspect of our everyday experience.

As when we encounter a major stressor, sometimes we become fragmented because our circumstances demand it. I learned my compartmentalization skills in seminary. It was easier for me to accomplish what I needed to both at home and at school by blocking out what was going on in the other arena. When I left the baby-sitter's house for my drive to school, in my mind the door to home closed and the door to seminary opened. When I was in one room, I tried not to think about what was going on in the other. As I returned to retrieve my children, seminary melted away and home became real again.

The more time passed, the better I got at compartmentalizing, and the more fragmented I became. I was two people living in the same body. What began as a coping strategy, effective in a particular time and place, became a life habit. So ingrained was this method of dealing with life that years later, when serving my first church in Indiana, I did not recognize the voice or even the name of a familiar colleague when she called my home. I was in my "home room" and had shut the door to my "work room." She did not fit in my home context and therefore, I could not even place her in my world at all. That was an eye-opener!

Type 2: When All Parts Fail

The other type of fragmentation, being pulled apart by many competing demands, is also a struggle for many women. Recently my youngest daughter, Hannah, introduced me to an insightful illustration of this affliction: a children's book called *Parts*, by Tedd Arnold. In a series of humorously illustrated scenes, a little boy is convinced his body is falling apart. He has numerous bits of evidence, such as a few hairs in his comb, some fuzz in his belly button (his stuffing was coming out after all!), and a loose tooth. In a moment of panic, he screams, "The glue that holds our parts together isn't holding me!!!"[1] That's what this type of fragmentation feels like—the glue that is supposed to hold our parts together just isn't holding anymore.

Each of us can become fragmented in this way. What woman has not experienced the exhaustion of having said yes too many times? "Sure, I can get the presentation done by Tuesday." "Of course I can bake five dozen cookies for the bake sale." "Work late? No problem." "Drive on the field trip? I'd love to." We are masters at overextending ourselves. We commit, commit, commit, then dash about frantically trying to squeeze productivity out of every available minute.

I know this firsthand. Frequently I'm able to get my work done only because I'm willing to take it with me wherever I go. I grab thirty minutes of reading or writing during Nathan's piano lesson, thirty more during Hannah's, and another thirty during Nathan's drum session. I can complete an hour of work on the sidelines at soccer practice or in the bleachers at gymnastics. Recently John took me on a weekend getaway to Chicago with one stipulation—no work. If I wanted to go I would bring pleasure reading only and *no laptop computer*. What a glorious weekend it turned out to be!

An Outside Perspective

As in my seminary experience, some of us become fragmented out of necessity. We divide ourselves in order to cope. Others of us become fragmented in a more casual way, often without even realizing it. Slowly, almost imperceptibly, we pile things on our plate—responsibilities, commitments, projects. Then suddenly we realize that we simply cannot do all the things we've agreed to do—at least not without risking our sanity.

Sometimes an outside perspective helps us identify this tendency. Several years ago I received a call from a woman at the *Asbury Herald*, an Asbury Seminary magazine, asking to interview me for an article on women in ministry. She caught me as I was unloading my groceries (thank goodness for cordless phones!) and we set up a time for the official interview. When the article arrived, I was in for some realization.

It's Tuesday. Kim and her husband, John, awaken their children, help get them dressed, have breakfast and then race out the door. John heads to his medical practice, but before Kim's off to work, she takes the kids to school. First stop—the elementary school. Nathan, a fourth grader, and Maggie, a second grader, are dropped off. Second stop—the local "Mother's Day Out" program and preschool where five-year-old Hannah attends. After depositing the children, Kim has just enough time to make it to the church . . . for the 9:15 staff meeting.

Once the meeting ends at about 10:45, Kim hurries to the elementary school to pick up Nathan. She has one hour to eat lunch with him and take him to his piano lesson. While Nathan's learning his scales, Kim pulls out one of her research books and starts reading. Every moment counts and she takes advantage of them. Once the piano lesson has ended, Kim and Nathan head back to school where Nathan goes to class and Maggie comes out. The same lunch time/piano hour is repeated with her. At 1 p.m. Maggie goes back to school and Kim has until 3 p.m. to work on church-related business or household duties. At 3 p.m., the kids are home. Now it's time to complete the family activities: dinner, homework, reports of the day, etc.

At 6 p.m., it's time to head back out the door and take the girls to gymnastics.

By 8 p.m. everyone's home and preparing for bed.

For Kimberly Dunnam Reisman, an associate pastor at Congress Street, U.M.C., each Tuesday is the same. And Monday, Wednesday, Thursday and Friday aren't too different. It's become a great balancing act between ministry in the church and ministry at home.[2]

Who is this woman? I wondered as I read. *She's running everywhere and barely has time to think! She really should try to pace herself better.* This was good advice if I could follow it consistently. But even to this day, that is my struggle.

Many Selves

There are times when the divisions we experience come from our desire to cope with the demands of our lives. There are others when the sheer volume of our responsibilities is what splinters us. There are also times when the fragmentation we feel comes from our sense of self or *selves*: for whatever reason, many of us feel like a jumble of different selves within one body. We have the self that carries all the good memories and lessons, and a self that carries all the negative baggage as well. We have the self that nurses all the hurts in our lives, keeping them as fresh as when they first occurred, and the one that nurses other people's hurts, seeking to bring healing and reconciliation. We have the self that looks out for us, and the one that looks out for others. You get the idea. Fragmentation occurs when all the different selves that make up *myself* will not or cannot talk to each other.

As a college student, I led a pretty wild lifestyle. That time was filled with lots of fun and excitement, but also with some things I'd rather forget or at least keep quiet. When I entered the ministry I worried that my wild days would come back to haunt me. I tried to push them away, pretend they didn't happen. I wrongly believed that if I acknowledged the fullness of my past, I wouldn't be able to minister.

Yet those years and all they contained have made me who I am. Some of the most powerful moments of my life and ministry have occurred when I have allowed myself to reconnect with that past—when I have allowed my college self to speak to my minister self. My life in college does not make up all of me, but it is a part of me, a part that needs to be heard now and again if I'm to be the whole and Christ-centered person God intended me to be.

In his book *Dancing at My Funeral*, Maxie Dunnam describes this experience in his own life in part of a poem, then tells what he's learned.

> To know myself
> as a weakling—
> impotent to resist
> as a giant
> with untapped strength
> as a mixture and a mess
> a hero and a coward
> a laugher and a crier
> a talker and a listener
> a reconciler and a fighter
> a lover and a hater
> To know the we in me. . . .

I've learned that I have many selves, including some negative selves. I seek to recognize and experience all of these selves so that they can have communication one with the other and thereby become integrated into my whole self. Self-pity, or self-condemnation, or self-rejection comes when I see one of my "little" selves as the whole me. If my greedy self emerges (as it often does) to drive me to seek "things" which I didn't have in childhood, I have to be careful not to see that as the entire me—likewise, when I am jealous, lustful, possessive, hateful. No one of these is my whole self. I am a kingdom of selves. Recognizing this, I am able to move toward wholeness.[3]

Regardless of how we become fragmented, the result is the same. We are pulled apart. We are a jumble of pieces rather than a whole, integrated being. We either cannot find our center because our lives are full of too many distractions, the demands of our circumstances cause us to build barriers, or our pasts have placed too many layers of "self" upon us. But God did not intend for us to live as a jumble of pieces; rather God desires wholeness.

A Picture of Wholeness

Leontyne Price is a great singer who time and again thrilled audiences at the Metropolitan Opera. As a black woman growing up in Laurel, Mississippi, she overcame poverty and deprivation to became a symbol of hope for millions of people. In the prime of her brilliant career she began to withdraw and become very selective about scheduling recitals. When an interviewer asked her why, she responded:

There are certain things in life that you have to have, because without them you are so uptight and tense that all the joy is gone from performing. Why, a few years ago I couldn't have sat here talking with a critic, let alone talked about myself. I even used to assume the conductors knew more than I did. Now, I feel I have recaptured the joy of singing, the feeling that courses through your body when you know the tone is right and your whole being vibrates with it.[4]

Leontyne Price sounds like a woman who has discovered her center and has chosen to order her life around it. That is what God desires for us. God wants us to experience the "feeling that courses through your body when you know the tone is right and your whole being vibrates with it."

The Spoke of Temperance

Fragmentation is the archenemy of wholeness. It blocks us from getting the tone right. Remember temperance? Temperance is the ordering of our souls that keeps them free by helping us avoid bondage to a particular impulse or appetite. Temperance, another word for balance, is the virtue that allows us to set priorities and goals, to employ the concept of delayed gratification, and to make sacrifices for what we want. When we order our souls by exercising temperance, we are able to make wise judgments about what we should do or not do in order to reach our goals. We become willing to make choices—even hard choices—because we know that they will enhance our well-being.

For Christ followers, temperance is not simply something we seek for our own sakes, although that is a wonderful benefit. There is a goal to that soul ordering: love, love of God, and love of neighbor. Fragmentation, in both its forms, blocks not only our ability to order our souls and achieve the balance and wholeness we desire, it blocks us from our goal of love.

Fragmentation turns us inward. We may believe that we have an outward focus: after all, we are so involved in so many things, how could we be focused on ourselves? But the reality is that when we are fragmented, we are turned inward, not toward our center, but toward the many parts that are pulling us asunder or toward the one particular aspect that dominates our life. The task of juggling all the various parts of ourselves consumes our energy and focus, or the effort involved in serving our dominant element saps our strength.

God desires not that we live with fragmentation and inner division but that we live with wholeness and integrity, and God will support us in our quest for it. In Paul's letter to the church at Thessalonica, he reminded them of God's desire and promise: "May the God of peace make you holy through and through. May you be kept in soul and mind and body in spotless integrity until the coming of our Lord Jesus Christ. He who calls you is utterly faithful and he will finish what he has set out to do" (1 Thess. 5:23-24, adapted from PHP).

According to the Random House dictionary, one definition of integrity is "the state of being complete or undivided." Webster's calls it "intactness." We reach that state of wholeness by exercising temperance—begin to evaluate our priorities, embrace delayed gratification, and make sacrifices where necessary. In doing this with care and prayer, we naturally move toward Christ, our center. Then, no matter how many selves we discover, how many demands impinge upon us, or how strongly one part of us seeks to dominate, we have a foundation upon which we can stand, intact and whole.

Like the concept of "good enough," temperance, that tool of intactness, is another spoke in the wheel of our life leading from our center in Christ to the place where the rubber hits the road. The spoke of temperance works with the spoke of "good enough" to provide a stable wheel to support our sometimes wobbly ride through the streets of our competing commitments, protecting us from veering out of control or losing our balance altogether.

T H R E E

Who Am I Today?:
The Tyranny of Roles

e all play several roles even over the course of a day. The problem with roles is that they pigeonhole us. They turn us into slaves of the expectations that others have of the role we have taken on. They encourage an external rather than an internal focus and obstruct our ability to understand ourselves and therefore, to live as Christ-centered women.

Mary Ellen Ashcroft hit the nail on the head when she wrote:

> Roles are great in the theater. And at times we have to play them in the rest of life. But when we spend too much time playing different roles, it can rob us of our sense of the person at the center of the roles. Instead of the integrated self, we find ourselves disintegrated. Soon we can't find that person at all.[1]

If concentrating on roles is such a hindrance to our personal growth and centeredness, why do we give them such attention? The simplest answer is because it is easier to focus on our roles than on ourselves. Devoting ourselves to our roles requires little self-exploration. Society has mapped out numerous expectations for a wide variety of roles. These expectations are fairly well known, so we can follow the basic script without much introspection. The process of understanding who we are as particular, authentic persons, uniquely created by God, takes a great deal more effort.

While the process of understanding who we are can be difficult for anyone, our inclination to accept expert opinion rather than trust our own inner voices frequently intensifies our struggle with self-knowledge. Throughout history, men have been giving authoritative advice on all kinds of issues, from medicine to psychology to theology, and women have taken that advice as gospel truth, even when the advice made no sense in relation to our inner voice or instincts. Worse still, over time many women have lost touch with that sense of interior instinct, so loud were the voices of the experts.

Only recently have we realized that all of this advice has been dispensed not necessarily from an objective *human* perspective, but from a subjective *male* perspective. A dangerous example of this is in the area of medical research, where for years the testing groups were composed only of men because the male body was considered the "norm." That left women open to the risky prospect of undertaking medical therapies deemed safe, but whose effects on the unique elements of women's bodies were actually completely unknown. Apparently this did not seem to be an issue for anyone in the world of medical research until the last decade of the twentieth century.[2]

How We Look v. Who We Are

Tied closely to our inclination to trust others more than ourselves is our tendency to view ourselves from the outside. It is our appearance, not who we are, that is important. John and I have a running joke about "trophy wives." He started the joke after attending one of his first medical meetings and noticing the seemingly common occurrence of older doctors showing up with very young, beautiful, second wives. He calls me his trophy wife with pride and appreciation when we're decked out in our best for a special event, but with good-humored sarcasm when I'm at my worst—sick and in bed, gardening and covered with dirt, bleary-eyed from being up all night with one of our children. Because I know my husband, we can share this joke.

At a deeper level, though, it is not very funny, because it highlights society's overarching emphasis on a woman's appearance. Rather than urging us to explore who we are as persons, society urges us to focus on how we look to the men around us. We heed the message and grow up believing that our beauty, or lack thereof, is our defining characteristic. So we cram our feet into high-heeled shoes, spend enough money on makeup, creams, and lotions to fund a small nation, and shave every visible hair from our bodies. The hair we leave on our heads we cut, dye, perm, or relax so much it's amazing it doesn't fall out by the time we reach fifty.

The antidote, self-exploration, takes effort, and society discourages women from making the effort to increase their self-understanding; therefore it is easier to fall back on the roles society provides. At a deeper level, however, many women fear what they might discover about themselves if they were to look too closely. Often we harbor the fear that if we were truly known we would not be loved. That is why we are so inclined to try to earn, through role playing, love from others and from God. We can't seem to grasp the possibility that people and God might love us simply because we are the persons we are—not because of what role we play in life.

Role v. Relationship

Not only does our preoccupation with roles prevent us from knowing ourselves, it also impedes us in developing relationships. Relationship lies at the heart of the majority of roles we undertake. Becoming a wife, a mother, or even an employee involves being in relationship with another person. If we are not careful, we can forget that it is the relationship that is primary, not the role.

The church has not always helped us with this distinction. In teaching biblical truths, it has sometimes focused more on roles rather than the relationships that ground them. This has often been true in the case of the relationship between husbands and wives. Consider the way we've interpreted the following scripture.

Be subject to one another out of reverence for Christ. Wives, be subject to your husbands as you are to the Lord. For the husband is the head of the wife just as Christ is the head of the church, the body of which he is the Savior. Just as the church is subject to Christ, so also wives ought to be, in everything, to their husbands.

Husbands love your wives, just as Christ loved the church and gave himself up for her, in order to make her holy by cleansing her with the washing of water by the word, so as to present the church to himself in splendor, without a spot or wrinkle or anything of the kind—yes, so that she may be holy and without blemish. In the same way, husbands should love their wives as they do their own bodies. He who loves his wife loves himself. For no one ever hates his own body, but he nourishes and tenderly cares for it, just as Christ does for the church, because we are members of his body. "For this reason a man will leave his father and mother and be joined to his wife, and the two will become one flesh." This is a great mystery, and I am applying it to Christ and the church. Each of you, however, should love his wife as himself, and a wife should respect her husband. (Ephesians 5:21-33)

This word to the Ephesians, though filled with seemingly troublesome language, points to a particular relationship that is to ground all other relationships—the relationship between Christ and humanity. We are to be subject to each other, to treat each other with the same sacrificial love and care that Christ has shown us. So far, so good—we can understand that. But when we move to the marital relationship it suddenly gets sticky. We hear the words "be subject" or "submit to" and immediately conjure up images of women in roles devoid of power or opportunity or personal growth. We hear "the husband is the head of the wife" and immediately see men in roles of unfettered power, ruling with iron fists. The roles we create in our imaginations become so magnified and distorted that we cease to see that it is not a role but a *relationship* that Paul holds up as the ideal to be modeled.

At the heart of this passage is the emphasis on comparing our marital relationships to the relationship we have with Christ. When I come into relationship with God through Jesus Christ and recognize the love that God has for me, I desire to place God at the center of my life—to orient myself around that radical gift of love shown in the life, death, and resurrection of Jesus. My relationship with my husband should mirror that. When I recognize my husband's love for me, that love should become a central part of my life—not an afterthought or pleasant extra or luxury—but a pivotal element of the way I live my life.

From this perspective, it is not the wife who has the most difficult challenge, for wives are simply reacting with gratitude and love to a love that is offered to them. Rather it is the husband who has the greater challenge, for he must love as Christ loved. "Husbands love your wives, just as Christ loved the church and gave himself up for her." That is a rigorous demand! The love that Christ offers the church is a sacrificial love, a love that loses itself on behalf of the other person. If husbands are to love that way, they must model their lives after the one who came not to be served but to serve, and to give his life as a ransom for many.

Paul offers not a disturbing word here, but a model for happy, holy marriage! Relationships between husbands and wives are not the only arena in which a preoccupation with roles hinders attention to relationships. For women, this often occurs with motherhood as well. Many of us suppose our children are products by which others judge our success at the role of mother. I still remember the day the nursery worker at my first church told me about an incident with my youngest daughter, Hannah, who was then about two. Hannah loved this woman and obviously felt very comfortable around her because one day she leaned over and whispered in a confidential tone, "Marge, I farted."

The woman in the nursery got a tremendous kick out of telling this story, and I admit I thought it was pretty funny myself. But in the back of my mind lurked this powerful sense that I had failed in some small way as a mother. It was as though when this story began to circulate (as I knew it would), my image as a mother who successfully taught her children to be polite in all circumstances (couldn't she have just said "passed gas" or better still, not said anything at all?) would never be as pristine as it was before.

When we view motherhood as a role rather than as a relationship, the stress involved increases exponentially. For most of us, the relationship is challenging enough without adding the extra baggage of image.

And focusing on the role of motherhood rather than the relationship between mother and child affects both parties. If our entire life is ordered around the *role* of mother, then as our children need us less and eventually leave us altogether, the source of our focus is gone. We are left with nothing but the remnants of the role for which we gave our life and lost our identity. It is no wonder so many women enter a crisis period when their children grow up and move away. This skewed view of motherhood affects children as well, planting within them the mistaken notion that women exist to serve and cater to their every need.

Focusing on the relationship that grounds motherhood moves us closer to balance and wholeness. When our children grow up and become independent, although the relationship has changed, it remains. In addition, we keep our identity—we are more than moms. Our children also benefit. Rather than seeing a model of self-denial, they see a well-rounded model for their own personhood. They see that it is important to pursue your own goals while supporting the goals of the people you love. When the *relationship* of motherhood is primary, we nurture ourselves as well as our children.

The Spoke of Self-Discovery

If we are to find our center and discover the wholeness God intends for us, we must at some point let go of our fear of knowing ourselves and grab onto the unconditional love of God.

This leads us to another spoke, that of self-discovery. As women we have not often been encouraged to undertake the effort involved in knowing ourselves. We've been told that working to find out who we are, to make any effort toward self-knowledge, is selfish or self-indulgent. We falsely assume that acknowledgment of the self is the same thing as preoccupation with the self. Christ-following women are at a marked disadvantage in this area. We have a long history of negative connotations regarding the self: it is to be lost or crucified, not discovered or recognized. Yet self-knowledge is crucial to finding our center and ordering our lives around it. Without a sense of who we are as persons, we will never be able to discover who we are in relation to God or those around us. And we will inevitably fall back into the trap of role playing.

As Mary Ellen Ashcroft said, roles are good in the theater, but not every day of our lives. Discovering our uniqueness as persons and the importance of the relationships in which we find ourselves is always a healthier, more balanced approach to living.

The task that lies ahead for each of us is to look within ourselves, even though it may be difficult, to gain a better sense of who we really are beneath the roles we accept. There, if we look closely enough, we will discover that we are the one-of-a-kind creations of a God who loves unconditionally. That realization is a pivotal step in moving toward our center and embracing the balance and wholeness that it brings; the spoke of self-discovery helps us live from that center.

Part Two

*Putting Christ–Centeredness
to Work*

FOUR

❧

The Search for Our Center: Discovering Who We Are

e have brought to light society's myths that block our journey toward balance and centeredness. We have understood how to replace the arbitrary, external expectations of the world with our own perception of "good enough." We have unveiled the internal impediments we place on our movement toward centeredness, resolved them with the tool of temperance, and we have highlighted the importance of discovering who we are as unique persons created by God. We may embrace all that we have discussed up to this point, but before we can actually put it into practice, we need to have a sense of who we really are. Without this, not only will we be unable to attain a clear sense of what is good enough and so fall prey to myths, fragmentation, and the tyranny of roles, we will be unable to discern where our center actually lies. Herein lies the crux of the entire enterprise. Without a clear awareness of our center, our journey toward balance and wholeness is doomed.

We ask this question, "Who am I?", aloud or silently all the time. As a pastor I encounter many people who are visiting our church for the first time. Frequently I initiate conversation by saying, "I don't believe we've met; my name is Kim Reisman." As we shake hands the person will usually offer his or her name in return, understanding immediately that my implied question is "Who are you?" Giving our name is the first step in letting someone know who we are. It's also the first step in understanding for ourselves who we are.

Names Are Important

Names identify us in relation to other people. When we name something or someone, we become connected in a unique way; we gain an entirely new dimension of relating. Many of us know the story of Helen Keller who, as a toddler, was stricken with an illness that left her blind, deaf, and mute. In our modern world it is hard to imagine, but at the end of the nineteenth century these handicaps completely cut off Helen from the world. Many people thought Helen was an idiot; though her parents believed otherwise, they had no way of reaching her or discovering what gifts lay within. Helen was locked in an isolated world of silence and darkness, becoming what she described as a "Phantom living in a world that was no-world."[1] This was the life of Helen Keller until she discovered names.

On April 5, 1887, as her teacher signed the word and pumped water into her hand, Helen's world suddenly broke open. She realized that this cool, wet stuff had a name—water. She realized that no matter where she found the stuff, the name would remain the same, it would always be water. Keller described this momentous event in the life of her "phantom" self:

> Suddenly Phantom understood the meaning of the word, and her mind began to flutter tiny wings of flame. Caught up in the first joy she had felt since her illness, she reached out eagerly to Annie's ever-ready hand, begging for new words to identify whatever objects she touched. Spark after spark of meaning flew through her mind until her heart was warmed and affection was born.[2]

Names were the key to Helen Keller's new world, providing her a connection and a means of relating. Names are what prompted that flutter of tiny wings of flame and produced spark after spark of meaning.

They hold the same power for us. Names open up the world to us and our own names connect us to that world. We remember our relationships and connections each time someone uses our name. My full name is Kimberly Lynn Dunnam Reisman. When people call me "Pastor Kim" (a title I had never heard before coming to Indiana), I know immediately that we are connected through the church. When they call me "Pastor" or "Reverend Reisman," just as quickly I understand that we are not yet connected, a relationship has not yet been born.

We can see other connections in our names. Reisman is my married name—it is one of the things that connects me to my husband and children. It also connects me to the larger world. I am quickly aware of my context when I hear someone address me as "Mrs. Reisman." Without thinking I know that the person is either a child or a stranger. The world "Mrs. Reisman" lives in primarily involves her children and their friends and activities, their school and teachers.

Dunnam is my maiden name. It is one of the things that connects me to my parents and brother and sister. Not as many people know this name, this layer of my personhood. People usually discover it later—after we have established relationships and there is a sense of closeness.

Then there is Kimberly Lynn—or just Kim—the closest indicator of me. This is the name that connects me to myself. When I am called Kim, I know that the other person knows me. Kimberly Lynn is the foundation for all my other names. Pastor Kim could not exist without Kimberly Lynn. Mrs. Reisman would be nothing without Kimberly Lynn. Even Dunnam couldn't stand well alone without Kimberly Lynn to hold it up.

Rather than pointing to my relationship with other people, Kimberly Lynn is the name that points to who I am in my innermost being. Others will never know me until they know that name. As I seek to find my center, as I seek to answer the question, "Who am I?" I must first follow the direction in which that name points. Only that name points inward to the heart of who I am rather than outward to all my other connections. Who am I? I am Kim. Who are you?

God's Names

God understands the importance of naming—that names point to the heart of things. This shouldn't surprise us; God has been in the business of naming since the beginning. When creating the heavens and the earth, God named them (Gen. 1:1-10). When creating animals and birds, God "brought them to the man to see what he would call them; and whatever the man called every living creature, that was its name" (Gen. 2:19).

The biblical witness of God's activity in the world is most powerful when it describes events of God's naming and renaming. Remember the story of Jacob? His name meant "deceiver." He was the second of twin boys born to Isaac and Rebekah. Because he was second, he wasn't entitled to his father's birthright, but he wanted it badly. So he tricked his blind father into thinking that he was his older brother, Esau, and stole his blessing (Gen. 27).

Later in life, Jacob was alone in the evening when a man came to him and they wrestled all night long. When the man was unable to overpower him, he wrenched Jacob's hip.

> Then he said, "Let me go, for the day is breaking." But Jacob said, "I will not let you go, unless you bless me." So he said to him, "What is your name?" And he said, "Jacob." Then the man said, "You shall no longer be called Jacob, but Israel, for you have striven with God and with humans, and have prevailed." (Genesis 32:26-28)

God's naming continues throughout all the encounters with God's people. Whenever God calls out to someone, God calls out a name: Noah, Moses, Deborah, Saul, Peter. God reaches out to each of us, calling us by the name that points to who we are in our innermost being. And having called out to us, God claims us and pledges to remain with us through it all.

> But now thus says the LORD, he who created you,
>   O Jacob, he who formed you, O Israel:
> Do not fear, for I have redeemed you;
>   I have called you by name, you are mine.

When you pass through the waters, I will be with you;
and through the rivers, they shall not overwhelm you;
when you walk through fire you shall not be burned,
and the flame shall not consume you.

(Isaiah 43:1-2)

God doesn't stop the naming activity with us. God is willing to name himself as well. The most memorable event of God's self-naming occurred with Moses. God appeared to Moses in the burning bush and told him that he would lead the Israelites out of slavery in Egypt. Moses was dumfounded and doubted his ability to undertake such a task. God assured him that he would be with him. Again, Moses protested and asked God who he should tell the Israelites was sending him (a polite way of asking, "Who are you?"). In response, God said, "I AM WHO I AM." He added, "Thus you shall say to the Israelites, 'I AM has sent me to you'" (Exod. 3:14).

Neither of these was very concrete. Thank goodness, God continued, "Thus you shall say to the Israelites, 'The LORD, the God of your ancestors, the God of Abraham, the God of Isaac, and the God of Jacob, has sent me to you.' / This is my name forever, and this is my title for all generations" (Exod. 3:15). This was tangible naming. God didn't use philosophical jargon or abstract concepts. God placed himself right in the middle of the world, where the action was, where life was lived. God was not in far-off places but was intimately connected to *people*.

Moses received God's identification in both the abstract and the concrete: "I am who I am. I am the God of your ancestors, the God who is actively involved in the life of my creation; the God who is *in* the world—connected to persons—in the midst of their lives."

God wasn't satisfied to leave self-naming at that. God continued with the ultimate self-naming—Jesus. Jesus is the particular that makes the abstract concrete for us. Particulars are the way we can understand concrete concepts. For instance, we can't completely understand what the abstract concept of love is until we experience a particular lover. Love in the philosophical sense remains just that—an abstract, theoretical notion—unless it becomes real for us through an encounter with a particular person whom we can actually love. God is like love for us—an abstract theoretical notion—until there is a particular to make that notion real. For Christ followers, that particular is Jesus. Jesus puts people in touch with God in a unique and decisive way. Without particulars, universals remain profoundly unknown, so vague that they lack any meaningful substance for our lives.

As Christ followers, we believe that Jesus is the specific way that God has chosen to be identified. Jesus is the name God has given himself so that we may know who the I AM truly is, in order that the I AM might become *real* in our lives.

Jesus, as the particular who makes the abstract real, shows us who God is. "For God, who said, 'Let there be light in the darkness,' has made us understand that this light is the brightness of the glory of God that is seen in the face of Jesus Christ" (2 Cor. 4:6, NLT). When we look at Jesus, we discover what God is like. When we experientially know Jesus, we know God.

The Psalms: Naming Our Feelings

The place where our experience of God as real converges with our experience of who we really are, is the place in which we will discover the spiritual center for our lives. These two experiences don't necessarily come together for people in the same ways. Some of us may have a very real sense of God's presence in our lives, yet not have a complete understanding of who we are. Others of us may have a deep (yet hopefully always growing and evolving) awareness of ourselves but have not yet discerned God's activity in our lives. As I've said before, while our journeys may run parallel, they are always unique. Only you can know where you are on the road to centeredness.

If we earnestly seek a spiritual center for our lives, though, and regardless of where we are on the road toward it, we will each eventually need to come before God with our authentic selves. This is where we get to do the naming. We name our feelings before God, in whatever state we find ourselves. We name our anger. We name our fear. We name our joy. We name our sadness. It may seem difficult—or even inappropriate—but it is necessary. And you can be assured you won't be the first ever to have done it! A quick glance at the Psalms is evidence of that.

The writer of Psalm 121 experienced God as a source of protection and safety. When this person named him- or herself before God, it was from the perspective of security.

> I look up to the mountains—
>> does my help come from there?
> My help comes from the LORD,
>> who made the heavens and the earth!
> He will not let you stumble and fall;
>> the one who watches over you will not sleep.
>> > (Psalm 121:1-3, NLT)

In Psalm 8, we see a different self, one experiencing awe in the face of God's creation and praise for God's greatness.

> O LORD, our Sovereign,
>> how majestic is your name in all the earth!
> . . . When I look at your heavens, the work of your fingers,
>> the moon and stars that you have established;
> what are human beings that you are mindful of them,
>> mortals that you care for them?
> Yet you have made them a little lower than God,
>> and crowned them with glory and honor.
>> > (Psalm 8:1, 3-5)

In Psalm 23:1 the poet speaks from the perspective of inner peace, contentment, and closeness with God: "The LORD is my shepherd, I shall not want." We can find thanksgiving as well: "You have turned my mourning into dancing" (Psalm 30:11).

Yet not all of the writers called out to God from a positive perspective. Life is not always happy and we are not always confident and secure. Psalms 10 and 22 are examples of the depths many of us reach. The self named in Psalm 10 cried out in lonely anguish, "Why, O LORD, do you stand far off? / Why do you hide yourself in times of trouble?" (Ps. 10:1) And the voice calling out in Psalm 22 was near death, full of the agony of abandonment:

> My God, my God, why have you forsaken me?
> Why are you so far from helping me,
>   from the words of my groaning?
> . . . I am poured out like water,
>   and all my joints are out of joint;
> my heart is like wax;
>   it is melted within my breast;
> my mouth is dried up like a potsherd,
>   and my tongue sticks to my jaws;
> you lay me in the dust of death.
>
> (Psalm 22:1, 14-15)

Even as some of the poets railed against God's apparent absence, others longed for God to be with them and share their experiences: "As the deer pants for streams of water, so my soul pants for you, O God. / My soul thirsts for God, for the living God" (Psalm 42:1-2, NIV). Still others were aware that their lives were not what they should have been and they called out, "Have mercy on me, O God, because of your unfailing love" (Psalm 51:1, NLT).

The Psalms run the gamut of emotion and self-expression. From anger to praise, from sorrow to celebration, the writers of these wonderful songs approached God from the totality of their beings. We must do likewise. We must come before God with our authentic selves.

The Spoke of Authenticity

Recall the witness of Jesus: God is not waiting for us to be perfect. Whatever we are experiencing, whatever the depths of our pain and confusion, whatever the heights of our joy and delight, God desires that we share it. In that sharing, we not only become more aware of who we are at that moment, as well as in our broader life; we provide for ourselves yet another spoke to strengthen our wheel. This is the spoke of authenticity, of genuine connectedness with God.

This is a crucial spoke in our framework for balanced living. Having named ourselves before God, we not only become aware of the person we are, we also begin to discover the person God desires that we become. We open ourselves to the possibility that God will *re*name us. Remember what happened to Jacob? "Your name will no longer be Jacob. It is now Israel, because you have struggled with both God and men and have won."

And at that intersection—where we express through naming our genuine knowledge of ourselves and allow God to name us as God sees us, we find our center.

A story from Jesus' ministry further illustrates the importance of names. As his ministry progressed, Jesus began asking the disciples who they believed him to be. When they seemed to understand that he was the Messiah, Jesus took three of them up on a mountain.

> Jesus took Peter and the two brothers, James and John, and led them up a high mountain. As the men watched, Jesus' appearance changed so that his face shone like the sun, and his clothing became dazzling white. Suddenly, Moses and Elijah appeared and began talking with Jesus. Peter blurted out, "Lord, this is wonderful! If you want me to, I'll make three shrines, one for you, one for Moses, and one for Elijah."
>
> But even as he said it, a bright cloud came over them, and a voice from the cloud said, "This is my beloved Son, and I am fully pleased with him. Listen to him." The disciples were terrified and fell face down on the ground.
>
> Jesus came over and touched them. "Get up," he said, "don't be afraid." And when they looked, they saw only Jesus with them.
>
> (Matthew 17:1-8, NLT)

When Jesus encountered God on the mountain, God named him before the three disciples: "This is my beloved Son." God knew the whole person God intended Jesus to be, just as he knows the whole person he intends each of us to be. God announced it to everyone there. Yet, after this incredible event, the disciples still saw "only Jesus." Understandably, this "only" refers to the fact that Elijah and Moses had disappeared and Jesus was alone. At another level, though, it points to the person of Jesus that the disciples then saw. Gone was the name "beloved Son" and the dazzling persona proclaimed by God. What remained was Jesus, the simple person they were used to seeing.

This story of Jesus has become especially meaningful for me. Let me explain why.

The Real Me

Throughout my life, I have lived somewhat in the shadow of my father, Maxie Dunnam, a well-known United Methodist minister. At times this has been a wonderful blessing. I am sure that the opportunities I have had to interact with leaders within the larger church would never had happened were it not for my father. My first encounter with authorship came because he encouraged me to collaborate with him on a workbook project. Many people have extended me gracious hospitality because of their love for my father.

I have many reasons to feel fortunate to be Maxie Dunnam's daughter. Yet those very words, "Maxie Dunnam's daughter," have also been a heavy burden. Just as after the transfiguration Jesus' disciples saw "only Jesus," rather than the true person that God knew him to be, I have often wondered if people see the true person I really am—not Maxie's daughter, but Kim. That question led me to take my husband's name when I married, bucking my friends' practice of keeping their maiden names. With a new name, I could control who knew my family connection and gain an opportunity to establish myself.

Connected with the question of whether others saw the real me was the question of motive: I wondered, *Do you really care about me because I'm me, or do you just care about me because of the person I'm related to?* When I was younger I thought I was being oversensitive, simply an insecure adolescent. But as I got older I realized I had good reason to be inquisitive.

Shortly after being appointed to my first church in Lafayette, I began receiving warm calls from colleagues welcoming me into the area, some even resulting in a meeting for lunch. Little did I know that word of my "secret" had gotten out. After a seemingly appropriate amount of time, several of my colleagues, who had been so interested in getting to know *me*, revealed the true source of their interest—my father's preaching schedule. "We would love to have him preach for us. Would you ask him?" "I'm sure that if *you* asked him. . . . "

Then came the Walk to Emmaus®, a spiritual renewal movement within the United Methodist Church. This weekend retreat nurtures "pilgrims" in their faith through teaching, faith sharing, and other activities. For me this was a wonderful weekend of complete anonymity—no one even knew I was a clergyperson! What a remarkable experience of love—God's love transmitted through the love of others—for *me*.

Me—the unique, unrepeatable miracle of God that I finally understood myself to be (even though my parents told me that for longer than I could remember). Kim—not Maxie's daughter, not John's wife—not Nathan's, Maggie's, or Hannah's mother—but Kim. It was as though a bright light fell on me and I heard God's voice saying, "This is my beloved child." I knew who I was even if everyone else saw "only Kim."

The strangest part of this watershed weekend was that suddenly it didn't matter whether or not anybody knew whose daughter I was. Suddenly it didn't even matter if people might like me because of my father rather than because of me. I knew who I was. I was *Kim,* and I could accept my relationship to my father as the blessing that it is, step out of his shadow and into the light of God.

Not all of us have had to live in someone's shadow, but the story of Jesus' transfiguration has meaning for each of us as we seek to discover who we are. God sees us in ways that the world often fails to see. The person the world sees may appear unacceptable, or simply mundane. But the person God sees is never mundane, never unacceptable. The person God sees is unique and loved, always arrayed in dazzling clothing and named as a beloved child.

As we look within ourselves in order to answer the question, "Who am I?" we must look not just at what the world sees: a wife, a mother, a daughter, or simply a woman. We must look at what God sees, whom he believes and desires us to be: someone with unique gifts, someone loved and cared for—not because of what we do, or because of what we are—but simply *because* we *are*.

As we name ourselves honestly before God, we connect truly with God. We experience the helpful spoke of authenticity. We find our center. And our wheel turns smoothly.

FIVE

Discipleship and Centeredness:
Following Jesus' Call

oming before God with our authentic selves, and then experiencing God's claim upon our lives and renaming, are pivotal events in the search for our spiritual center. It is in these events that our sense of self converges with our sense of God as real. For Christ followers, Jesus Christ makes God real; thus Christ becomes our center when "his Holy Spirit speaks to us deep in our hearts and tells us that we are God's children" (Rom. 8:16, NLT).

When we place Christ at our center, the spokes that make up the wheel of our life change. Rather than depending on the wheel provided by the world, whose spokes include myths, fragmentation, roles, and an emphasis on "accomplishments" and "success," our wheel is discipleship, and its spokes are the concept of "good enough," temperance, self-discovery, and authenticity. Discipleship is responding to the call of Jesus in our lives. It involves listening to God's voice and following where that voice leads us.

If you are already a Christ-following woman, you are probably nodding your head and saying, "Of course, of course, let's just get on with it." But I don't believe it is as simple as it sounds. We have years of messages to contend with about what it means to be a disciple of Jesus who happens to also be a woman. Secular society as well as the church try to tell us how women should follow Christ. In our quest for balance and centeredness, we must be open to the voice of God in our lives, and we must be certain that it is God's voice we are heeding. We need to take a look at all those messages we receive, including the message of Jesus, so that we may be confident we are listening to the right voice as we seek to be disciples.

A Call to All

Jesus minced no words when calling people to follow, and Jesus called men and women alike. This is quite remarkable if we recall the situation women lived in during Jesus' time. Equally remarkable, given the circumstances, is the courage of the women who responded to Jesus' call. During Jesus' time, women were essentially treated as children. Their spiritual life was not their own but a vicarious experience mediated through their husbands and families. First-century Judaism and its society demanded that respectable women not be seen in public or speak to a man in public. It prohibited a woman from learning the Torah, following a rabbi, or making any ethical decisions apart from the guidance of her father or husband.

Of course Jesus knew about these restrictions. Like any adult male, particularly a rabbi (as Jesus was viewed throughout his ministry), Jesus knew that contact with women was supposed to be severely limited. Jesus knew about the prohibitions against talking with women or teaching them. Jesus knew that calling women to be his followers, touching them, or allowing them to touch him were forbidden. And Jesus knew that using them as illustrations in stories was pushing the envelope. Yet remarkably, Jesus talked with, taught, called, touched, was touched by, and included women anyway.

More remarkable still, they responded. Women followed Jesus faithfully, all over Galilee. According to all four of the Gospels, many women even undertook the week-long trip to be at the Lord's side in Jerusalem. That was a particularly daring move given the societal expectation of appropriate chaperoning by parents or a husband. It was Jesus' women disciples who stayed at the cross as he died. It was Jesus' women followers who saw where the Lord was buried. And it was the women who were the first to witness Jesus' resurrection.

Dorothy Sayers wonderfully describes the uniqueness of Jesus' call to women:

> Perhaps it is no wonder that the women were first at the Cradle and last at the Cross. They had never known a man like this Man—there never has been such another. A prophet and teacher who never nagged at them, never flattered or coaxed or patronized; who never made arch jokes about them . . . who rebuked without querulousness and praised without condescension; who took their questions and arguments seriously; who never mapped out their sphere for them, never urged them to be feminine or jeered at them for being female; who had no axe to grind and no uneasy male dignity to defend; who took them as he found them and was completely unself-conscious.[1]

A Personal Call

Though during his sojourn on earth, Jesus called members of both genders, Jesus also calls us individually. As we search for balance and centeredness, we do well to remember the story of Samuel and Eli. Eli was an old priest and Samuel a boy who served as his assistant. Twice one night Samuel heard a voice call to him. Thinking it was Eli, he went in to him and asked, "What do you need?" Eli sent Samuel back to bed because he had not called him. The third time Samuel went to Eli, the old priest realized that God was calling to Samuel. He told Samuel to lie down, and if he heard someone call again, he was to respond that he was listening. Sure enough, God called out to Samuel once more and Samuel responded (1 Sam. 3:1-10).

The importance of this story for us is the fact that while God had called Eli to be his priest and Eli had responded, when God called Samuel, Eli didn't hear. God's call to Samuel was personal, uniquely for Samuel's ears and no other's. Our callings are like that as well. God calls each person in a unique and personal way. When God speaks to you, that call is for your ears only. You may share it with others and you may journey with others as they respond to their unique callings, but God's call to you belongs to you.

As unique as our callings are, as Christ followers we belong to a community of faith. God calls not only individual disciples, but entire communities. We are called to follow Christ both in our personal endeavors and in the context of the believing community. Even as Samuel's call was for his ears only, Samuel didn't recognize it on his own. Eli helped him hear it. The community of faith can be a valuable source of help for us as well. As we seek to identify God's call in our lives we need to be careful that the call we are heeding is God's, not that of the world, of cultural myths, or even of our own wishes or assumptions. Even as we hear a call that is uniquely ours, we need sounding boards to help us discern both the call and our direction in following. The community of faith is a place where we can find those sounding boards. The community can provide important confirmation or significant words of caution for what we hear.

Called to Do What?

There is no doubt that Jesus called women as a gender and as individuals, but what did Jesus call them to do? That is where the story begins to muddy. Jesus' own words and actions were clear, but the jumble of voices that have been shouting at us ever since are not. For example, let's look at Jesus' interaction with Mary and Martha.

> Now as they went on their way, he entered a certain village, where a woman named Martha welcomed him into her home. She had a sister named Mary, who sat at the Lord's feet and listened to what he was saying. But Martha was distracted by her many tasks; so she came to him and asked, "Lord, do you not care that my sister has left me to do all the work by myself? Tell her then to help me." But the Lord answered her, "Martha, Martha, you are worried and distracted by many things; there is need of only one thing. Mary has chosen the better part, which will not be taken away from her."
>
> (Luke 10:38-42)

Much has been said about this passage over the years. Many of us are so familiar with it that we no longer really hear what it has to say. We've lifted Martha up despite this passage, even naming women's groups after her, so that we forget that Jesus actually had a very hard word for her, one that probably made her—and makes us—very uncomfortable.

At its most simplistic level, Jesus' call to Martha was to abandon the things that wasted her time and diverted her attention, the very things she believed were virtues for women. At a deeper level, this is Jesus' call to us as well. Jesus calls us to examine how we spend our time, to study what receives our attention. Christ challenges us to reassess those things because, like Martha, we may discover that they aren't as virtuous as we thought!

Jesus called women in the first century to take responsibility for their own lives. It was a call to grow up! Unlike his contemporaries, Jesus treated women like adults; he assumed an adult level of competence and demanded that they enter into spiritual reflection along with men. While society has progressed in numerous ways in the last two thousand years, we may not be as far along as we wish. Women are often still treated like children. I experienced this when an older member of the first church I served called me an "out-of-control little girl" simply because I was exercising assertive leadership. Before that, my year-long residency in clinical pastoral education required my evaluation by a committee of ministers. During that meeting this all-male committee implicitly questioned my competence when they asked if I believed my appearance would hinder my ability to be effective in ministry.

As women we must admit, though, we appreciate having someone look after us. Many times I have been grateful for the opportunity to defer a decision to someone else. Being responsible for ourselves, figuring things out on our own, can be difficult. But that is exactly what Jesus calls us to do. When we respond to Jesus' call, we realize that we are responsible for finding out what God is calling us to be. It lies with no one else to mediate God's voice; we are our own ears. This can be frightening.

Because listening to other voices can feel good and safe, many of us are slow to respond to Jesus' message to Martha. It pushes us too far from our comfort zones. We respond, "I like my spiritual life the way it is. I'm happy with the way I'm following right now. I'm satisfied with the role within the church that I've been given. Why do I have to reevaluate? Make Mary change, not me."

Idolatry: A Subtle Sin

In order to be centered, we must always reevaluate. We must take responsibility for our own spiritual growth by questioning ourselves to make sure we are listening to Jesus' voice. If we do not maintain a process of self-examination, we run a great risk of self-deception. Rather than following the unique calling of Jesus in our individual lives, we risk following the world's perception of Jesus' calling to all women's lives. We risk being led to believe we must be Ruths when Jesus wants us to be Orpahs. We risk being led to believe we should be Marthas when Jesus really wants us to be Marys.

Jesus' hard word to Martha challenged her both to grow up and to evaluate where her focus was—in essence, to abandon idolatry. Jesus was not calling Martha to be Susie Homemaker or even Superwoman, but to be a disciple.

So it is with us. Discipleship requires us not only to follow Jesus, it requires us to guard against idolatry. We too must ask: What is my center? Is it still Christ? To whom am I listening—to Jesus or to the world?

Jesus' interaction with the rich man illustrates this principle. This man was very devout and had kept all the commandments but felt compelled to ask Jesus if he had missed anything in his spiritual quest. Jesus responded unequivocally, Yes! Jesus told the man that he had missed the most important part—giving up all he had so he could follow. The man was devastated because he had great wealth. He wasn't willing to leave the security of all that the world had told him was important.

We are like the rich man. Like him, our idol may be money. Or it may be power or status, the fast track to corporate or financial success. Or our idols may subtler, as Martha's were: a clean house, perfect hostessing, home-cooked meals. They may be the distractions that we encounter in our daily life, the "small stuff" we're not supposed to sweat, but do.

A particularly subtle idol is the family. This is my point of struggle. It is culturally acceptable, even highly praised, to make the care of our families an all-engrossing task. What a sharp contrast to Jesus' teaching! Though given the opportunity, Jesus refused to promote family responsibilities above discipleship responsibilities. When a woman called out the common chorus, "God bless your mother—the womb from which you came, and the breasts that nursed you!" Jesus did not respond as we might expect. Christ replied, "But even more blessed are all who hear the word of God and put it into practice" (Luke 11:27-28, NLT). Discipleship over motherhood: what are we to make of that?

On another occasion someone told Jesus that his mother and brothers were waiting to see him. Jesus did not take this opportunity to teach about family members, nor even to give them attention. Instead Jesus simply said, "My mother and my brothers are those who hear the word of God and do it" (Luke 8:21).

Even more difficult are Jesus' words, "Whoever loves father or mother more than me is not worthy of me; and whoever loves son or daughter more than me is not worthy of me" (Matt. 10:37). That definitely puts things into perspective: our relationship with God comes before all else.

It is hard for us to hear such a sharp word against the very institution we have so elevated. It makes us wonder why Jesus was so harsh. Doesn't Jesus want us to care for our families and our children? Doesn't Jesus want us to raise our children well, nurturing them so they too will become good disciples? Of course he does. But Jesus is aware of our keen ability to be lured into idol worship. Because of that awareness, he spoke strongly and got our attention. We are frequently quick to condemn those who make idols of sex or power, but we must guard against family idolatry with as much vigilance. If we do not, Jesus' unique call to each of us will become fainter, drowned out by the noise of sporting events, carpools, and Teletubbies.

Time: The Priceless Resource

Along with challenging Martha to abandon idolatry, Jesus also let her know that she did not understand how important her *time* was. She was wasting her time and energy on all those details. Her time was more valuable than that! She should have been spending it wisely as Mary was, listening to and learning from Jesus. What a lesson that holds for us! If we are to lead balanced and centered lives, if we are to build our lives on the framework of discipleship, we must learn to value our time.

Through her actions, Martha was telling Jesus that the way Mary spent time, in spiritual study and reflection and theological conversation, was not valuable or productive. That is what the world tells us as well. The world would have us believe that time spent with God, time devoted to spiritual growth, prayer, or silent meditation, is wasteful. Jesus corrects both Martha and the world. Jesus tells us that what is really important is not productivity but faith, and the most valuable time of all is that spent in the nurture of faith.

Women have a great deal of difficulty with time. My husband has often told me that I need a lesson in time management. Maybe I do. But what really plagues women is not an inability to manage time. What plagues us is the difficulty we have in valuing it. Society tells us, and we often believe, that our time is simply not as valuable as men's time is. One of the more obvious ways society does that is with money. Society says, "Time is money," yet women are not paid as much as men, so our time must not have as much value.

Periodically I receive phone calls from charity organizations asking if I will help their fund-raising campaigns by sending letters to my neighbors. They insist that they will provide all the material, all I need to do is take a "little time" to fill in names on the letters, sign my name, stamp and address the envelopes, and drop them in the mail. I have no problem with this sort of campaign. In fact, if the cause were one that I felt Jesus was calling me to support, I would be happy to undertake the task. What I find annoying is that while these organizations always call me by name, they never call my husband. I suppose someone out there feels that Mrs. Reisman will have a "little time" but Mr. Reisman certainly will not.

If we are to be faithful disciples, we must guard against this devaluing of our time. If we are to remain centered, we have to turn a deaf ear to the cultural messages that tell us that our callings to spiritual nurture are not important.

The Spoke of Valuing Our Calling

These messages do not come only from the outside; we speak them to ourselves as well. As I write this, my children are on their spring break from school. Neither my husband's schedule nor the deadline for this book allowed a family vacation right now. I'm thankful that my church allows me to take time for study once a year; this gave me the opportunity to pack up the children and drive to my in-laws' home for a visit. The ground rules are that I work on the book while my children enjoy their grandparents.

My in-laws have done their part, with swimming outings each day, visits to the local children's museum, and even an opportunity to see David Copperfield perform his incredible illusions. I have been working diligently, but not without some guilt. Unfortunately, each day my children seem to conveniently forget the ground rules. While they readily accepted (with disappointment, but without a fight) that their father had to work, they haven't been so understanding with me. "I don't see what's so important about your work" has been their refrain as I leave each morning for the library. I have never heard them tell their father that! Or they ask, "Why can't you be with us?" I answer their questions as best I can, telling them that my work is important too, and then I leave, wondering if I should have spent less time on my book and more time with them.

Looking at it objectively, I know that my children are fine. They have had a wonderful time with grandparents they see only a few times a year. Intellectually I know that my decision to limit my work to part time affords them ample attention from me and that these four days of work are not going to scar them for life. Yet my guilt continues to flash with each reference to how much my children want me to stay home.

I do not believe I am alone in these feelings. We are all faced with competing demands on our time. It is in part because of those competing demands that we so desperately need to find our center in the first place. One writer speaks eloquently describes the source of my guilt over attending to my own work rather than spending time with my children:

> At the heart of this is the issue of whether a woman deserves to pursue her calling, whether she can claim the space and time, whether, in fact, her calling is really a calling from God and is important. She has to surmount what may seem like an incredible hurdle, and that is to say, "My time is important. My life is important. Not just as it is used to please and serve others. My calling is important. Even though I am not a man." A woman may not realize how revolutionary this idea is until she tries to implement it in her life. She will find herself apologizing to everyone—to the one she has hired to help her with the housework, to the child-care helper, to her children, to the school, to her church and perhaps most of all to her husband ("I'm sorry that it's leftovers again tonight." "I'm sorry the laundry is not done." "I'm sorry we're out of cookies.").[2]

This statement is compelling because it points to the fact that not only have we as women absorbed the message that our time is not valuable, we have gone one step further by failing to see ourselves as people who contribute through our own pursuits to the common good. As my dilemma suggests, it is often difficult for us to devote time to our personal callings. It is difficult not only because we question the value of those callings but because of two very pragmatic issues as well—the lack of uninterrupted time and available space.

Simply looking at the way houses are traditionally designed illustrates how little we value a woman's personal pursuits. Generally speaking, everyone in the family has a personal space except the wife and mother. Dens or studies have typically been the domain of men. Children have their bedrooms and playrooms or a family room. The whole family spends time in the kitchen, dining room, and living room. Where does a woman go when she wants to be alone?

Mary Ellen Ashcroft contends that "what women lack most often is the time alone to do what we are called to do."[3] We are the ones upon whom society places the demand to choose between home and self. Dorothy Sayers was right in pointing out that men are not required to choose between their family life and their jobs or personal callings; men get both.[4] It is the woman, particularly the married woman with children, who faces the difficulty of caring for her children while trying to nurture her own talents and gifts—not to mention providing emotional support for her husband. No wonder I find myself complaining to my husband that I need a wife!

If we are to find balance by centering our lives on Christ, we must counteract this devaluing of our time and personal pursuits. We must recognize that Jesus has called us and that following Jesus is valuable. We must reassert to ourselves and to others that our time and our pursuits are important, even when we are not actively working to serve or please others. Valuing our calling is another strong spoke on our wheel.

Six

To Find Our Niche:
Asking the Right Questions

ollowing Christ is the framework on which we build a balanced life. Jesus calls us to full discipleship, not a partial façade of discipleship that makes exceptions for us because we are women. Our sense of balance and wholeness is heightened when we listen to the voice of God, calling us in directions uniquely suited to our gifts and talents. We can feel it when we make decisions based not on what society tells us we should be or do, but on how those decisions fit with God's direction. Our sense of centeredness is strengthened when we become like Mary, sitting at Jesus' feet, drinking in every word, learning, growing, following.

When we accept discipleship as the framework for our lives and seek to follow the voice of God, as we value our calling, one of the first questions we face is, *"What* should I do?" Our answers will vary depending on our circumstances and gifts. Yet for all of us it is actually only a surface question. If we concentrate only on the "what" question, we risk missing an even deeper and more important question which is: "Why?"

Before we can truly answer "What should I do?" we must explore the question, "Why should I do it?" Why should I make this choice? If I am going to do this, why am I doing it? Many commitments compete for our attention. Unfortunately, there is no one answer for all of us. For instance, choosing to work outside the home will be right for some; choosing to remain home with the children will be right for others. Therefore, the question that needs our attention most is "Why?"

Asking "Why?" guards us against the idolatry that Jesus warned Martha about. It encourages ownership of our spiritual journey. When we ask why, we are taking responsibility for ourselves and our choices.

Asking "Why?" focuses our attention on our motives. Why am I making this choice? Am I making it because I believe God is leading me? Am I making it because it is what others expect of me?

Asking "Why?" calls attention to our view of our time. Why should I, rather than someone else, do this? Am I best suited to do this because of my gifts, or do I feel obligated to do it because I have the time?

Asking "Why?" centers us on Christ. It helps us find the right things to do—things that uniquely fit the talents Christ has given us, things that develop our discipleship.

I remember when I was preparing to increase my workload from quarter to half time. I was excited and ready to become more involved in ministry. At that same time, however, my son, Nathan, began struggling in school and was diagnosed with a learning disability. It was obvious that he would need both John's and my attention as he began adapting to his unique style of learning.

I was in a quandary. I had been convinced that the time was right to increase my involvement in ministry, but now I was torn—what should I do? As I began to pray for guidance, I also began asking myself the deeper "why" question. Why did I feel that the time was right to increase my workload? Was it my own need for a greater challenge? Was God leading me to make this change? Was God leading me to continue my current commitment at home? Why was it so important to me to change now?

One evening as I was finishing up my nighttime routine with Nathan, we were both lying in the quiet darkness. Suddenly I had an overwhelming sense of presence in the room. I sat up and looked around, expecting to see my husband, but no one was there. I realized immediately that I needed to focus and listen. As I sat in the stillness I saw that I knew exactly what I needed to do and why I needed to do it. God was leading me to continue at home, not increase my workload. Why? Because Nathan needed a solid, consistent presence at home and I was best suited to provide that. John and I had discovered early on that I had the better gift for school support, particularly where Nathan was concerned. I was more adept at providing homework help and learning strategies. While John has many other parenting gifts, he was easily frustrated in this regard.

But what was I to do about my work? I realized that God wasn't calling me to abandon my ministry. Delaying my increase in work time did not mean I was no longer following. It simply meant that God had slowed the pace. I had my entire life to minister to other people, but I had only these few short years to nurture and support my son.

That night I received the essential answers to my "why" questions. I should stay home because Nathan needed me. And I had desired to increase my workload because I was basically bored with my current responsibilities. When I weighed the two answers, Nathan's need and my boredom, I knew what I had to do and that God had led me to it.

Asking "What?"

Asking "Why?" before asking "What?" is crucial to our ability to faithfully follow Christ's leading in our lives. Attending to these questions securely places responsibility for our discipleship on our own shoulders, which is where Jesus wants it to be. It focuses us on the foundation for our choices, which is equally as important as the choices themselves and sometimes, even more. It reminds us that our center is Christ, who has created us to accomplish specific tasks.

In contemplating what those tasks may be, we must examine the abilities with which God has endowed us. Many women have great difficulty with this element of self-awareness. They do not see themselves as "gifted" and therefore cannot readily point to any particular "gift." Yet they miss one of the most obvious signals of giftedness, *enjoyment*. The things that we enjoy frequently involve areas in which we are gifted.

I love to write. I am also fairly good at it. The joy I receive from writing is an important element in my use of this gift. It is sad when women feel that God's assigning them something that they enjoy and do well would be "too good to be true."

One of the tragedies of our modern, secular age is that we have lost a sense of the Holy Spirit working in our lives. We have become so dependent on the scientific or rational explanation that we forget that sometimes God is simply alive and well and active in our lives. We dismiss our enjoyment of the things we do well rather than recognizing that joy as the working of the Holy Spirit urging us to take the things that we do well and use them for God's purpose. I have been guilty of this. I probably would have been content to privately enjoy my writing if a colleague hadn't suggested that quite possibly God blessed me with a love of writing because God wanted me to use it as a part of my ministry. *Write as a part of my ministry?* I thought. *What a luxury!* No—not a luxury, a necessary part of the way God intended to use me.

God has blessed each of us with a unique array of talents. God has blessed you with a love for something because God wants you to use it as a part of the way you follow. At a church I served is a group of women who love to sew—and they do so skillfully. They enjoy both the sewing and the fellowship they share. A long time ago, someone had the wonderful idea that God could use these women's hobby, so they began to meet once a week for several hours of sewing and visiting. It would be impossible to catalogue all the things they have made for others over the years, including diapers and blankets for the local crisis pregnancy center and schoolbags for children in Liberia. The equipment and supplies that at first could be stored in one small room of the church soon spilled out into another. These women have been meeting now on Wednesdays for years—all because someone made the connection between a need and a gift.

Developing an understanding of how we are gifted prepares us to discern specifically how we should follow Jesus. Sometimes it can mean moving into territory that makes us uncomfortable, or doing things that challenge us to develop our abilities more fully. But following Jesus never means taking on commitments for which we are completely unsuited. If we cannot carry a tune in a bucket, chances are that opera singing is not the way God is calling us. But remember—the scope of our abilities is always magnified by God's power. There is always room for God to use us to do great and tremendous things—things that we never thought we could do. Those great things, however, are often composed of many smaller things, things that *are* in our power to do.

What Is My Kingdom Niche?

Integral to answering the question of what we should do is the issue of power. If we follow Jesus, if we make Jesus the center of our lives and discover the balance and wholeness he offers, we must have a clear sense of our own power. While we may not always feel it, each of us has inner power. God's gift of power is the ability to achieve purpose.

Over the years society has tried to take away our sense of inner power. Sometimes it is by deception, by leading us to believe that our inner power must be political or economic to be valuable. At other times society attempts to take away our inner power by sheer force—economic, physical, emotional, or mental. Yet God has given each of us a gift of power and discerning it is crucial to discipleship and centeredness.

Discerning our ability to achieve purpose enables us to act boldly in the present and to worry less about the future. Helen Bruch Pearson describes this understanding: "(I have learned) to be less anxious about tomorrow when I have done what is in my power to do today."[1]

Do what you have the power to do today. What a wonderful phrase! Pearson takes it from the story of the woman who anointed Jesus' feet with oil and it is a dramatic statement of what our discipleship might look like. Let's look at the story.

> Jesus was at Bethany in the house of Simon the leper; he was at dinner when a woman came in with an alabaster jar of very costly ointment, pure nard. She broke the jar and poured the ointment on his head. Some who were there said to one another indignantly,

"Why this waste of ointment? Ointment like this could have been sold for over three hundred denarii and the money given to the poor"; and they were angry with her. But Jesus said, "Leave her alone. Why are you upsetting her? What she has done for me is one of the good works. You have the poor with you always, and you can be kind to them whenever you wish, but you will not always have me. She has done what was in her power to do: she has anointed my body beforehand for its burial. I tell you solemnly, wherever throughout all the world the Good News is proclaimed, what she has done will be told also, in remembrance of her." (Mark 14:3-9, JB)

Earlier in this book we explored the amazing nature of Jesus' call to women. Recalling the status of women in Jesus' time ought to stir within us great awe at the courage of this woman who came so boldly into Jesus' presence. A woman anointing Jesus! It was such a dramatic event that all four gospel writers felt compelled to include it in some form. While our tendency is to combine the accounts into one homogenous story, the reports are widely divergent. Scholars disagree about why this is so, but for our purposes highlighting the parallels and contrasts enhances the power of the story.

We frequently think of this woman as a prostitute, but Luke was the only one who described her that way: "a woman in the city, who was a sinner" (Luke 7:37). Yet Luke omitted any mention of costly ointment, of Jesus' words about the poor, or of his preparation for burial, which are integral to the other gospels' telling of this story. Luke's emphasis was on forgiveness, a sharp contrast to Matthew, Mark, and John, who focused on the preparation of Jesus for burial. These three writers all placed the incident in Bethany toward the end of Jesus' ministry. They also highlighted the complaints of the other men regarding the waste of the valuable ointment, described Jesus' defense of the woman, and related the way Jesus distinguished between the poor who are always present and himself, who would soon leave.

In all the Gospels, this woman acted boldly. She asserted herself enough to touch and anoint Jesus without asking. Some criticized her boldness, but Jesus defended her and obviously approved of what she had done. Again, in all the Gospels the men treated the woman badly. The men with Jesus were rude and indignant. Mark said that the guests were rude, Matthew said it was the disciples who were indignant, Luke attributed the mean-spiritedness to the host, Simon the Pharisee, and John saw Judas behave badly. The important element in all of this is simply that no one saw the goodness of this woman's action—except Jesus.

Looking specifically at Mark's story, the amazing quality of this woman's deed cannot be overestimated. To anoint Jesus in this way was revolutionary behavior. Remember the social constraints and protocol we discussed earlier. First of all, the invited guests were all men—no woman would be present because Jewish custom prohibited women from entering a dining room where men were gathered. This woman crashed the party! Because the guests reclined on low couches around a table, the woman had to stand close behind Jesus in order to anoint him. The scene would have been extraordinary to witness, shocking, in fact—a woman standing over Jesus performing a dramatic act of hospitality, one that was usually reserved for the host.

What kind of response do we see to this extravagant gesture? Disdain, mostly, which points to a complete lack of understanding about what Jesus might have been going through. By the time this story occurs, Jesus had already predicted his death on three different occasions. The grief Jesus must have felt knowing what was to come must have been tremendous. Yet none of the guests seemed aware that Jesus was experiencing turmoil. No one made the connection between the woman's act and Jesus' impending death. It appears that the only people who recognized tragedy on the horizon were the woman and Jesus. In contrast to the disciples, this woman's act indicated her depth of understanding.

The Spoke of Recognizing Your Power

What are we to make of this scene? To get its full impact we need to recognize what is taking place in Mark's overall story. The Passover Feast, one of the holiest holidays in Judaism, was only two days away. Because of the significance of this holiday, people from all over had converged in Jerusalem. When Jesus arrived with the disciples and all the others, including many women, the city was buzzing with activity and excitement. Remember the cheers and people waving palm branches? But not everybody was in a good mood. Jesus made the religious leaders nervous. Jesus threatened their security, their status in Jewish society. Jesus questioned their authority and privilege and spoke harshly, humiliating them in public. They were not happy to see the Lord.

Even as the religious leaders were becoming more agitated, the disciples were becoming more confused. In Mark's Gospel, more than any other, the disciples just did not get it. They could not seem to recognize the true purpose of Jesus' ministry. Despite the fact that Jesus had told them three times that he must suffer and die, they continued to focus on the worldly aspects of his leadership: Jesus was the Messiah, the one who would establish a new kingdom for the Jews. Jesus wouldn't die; he would rule! Jesus' continued predictions just made the disciples increasingly anxious. They began to protest against him and argue amongst themselves. Who was the greatest? Who would receive the most honor?

I cannot imagine how frustrated and isolated Jesus must have felt in the midst of all the bickering and misunderstanding, knowing that the end was near and those closest to him were still unaware. Simon's invitation to dinner must have come as a welcome distraction. Yet in the middle of this dinner a woman intruded, abruptly, brashly, disrupting everything. Her bold entrance alone was probably enough to send the men through the roof in shock and anger, but then she went even further. She broke open the jar of ointment she was carrying and poured it on Jesus' head! What an outrage! How dare she be so foolish and impulsive? What a waste of money! Pure nard—one of the costliest ointments available—was worth a year's wages for a laborer.

Helen Bruch Pearson eloquently describes this daring woman:

A solitary figure, the woman was as bold and unashamed as she was tender and compassionate. Whether the woman had met Jesus before is unimportant. It was what she did in the unsolicited act of anointing that remains unforgettable. Apparently she was familiar with his teachings and took seriously the message about the new age that Jesus proclaimed—where all the old values would be turned upside down. Perhaps she had heard about the announcements he made about his own death and the plans of the chief priests and scribes. Perhaps her faith enabled her to discern the gravity of the situation. Whatever prompted her action, the woman willingly went against the accepted place of women in her religion and culture, for she realized that the time to do something for Jesus was soon to be no more. Out of her resources and possessions, she did what she had the power to do. She poured a senseless amount of precious perfumed ointment over Jesus' head.[2]

What a profound and intimate moment this must have been. Jesus didn't rebuke the woman or even move. Jesus simply sat and allowed her to act out her devotion, to offer her gift. Jesus accepted not only her behavior but also who she was as a person. In this silent acceptance, Jesus received this woman's gift, blessing it with the deep respect and reverence it deserved.

What a contrast between Jesus' response and that of the other guests! The disciples had been with Jesus for a long time. They had heard the preaching and teaching; they had seen him reach out to the outcast and unfavored. They had heard Jesus predict his fate, yet seemed unaware of his fatigue or anguish. Jesus must have been very disappointed to have to reprimand them yet another time. Once again, they could not see past their own worldly pursuits. As with so many other things, it was only later that the disciples recognized the significance of this woman's act of ministry with Jesus.

Jesus told the guests that this woman's remarkable act would be remembered wherever the good news was proclaimed. We need to remember this woman as we seek centeredness and balance in our lives because of the model she gives us for discipleship. She did what she had the power to do. She gave what was uniquely hers to give. We must do the same. We may not be able to do very much, or we may be able to do a great deal. The amount is irrelevant. God asks only that we do what we have the power to do.

Recognizing our inner power adds another spoke to our wheel. When we seek to be mature followers of Christ, we place Christ at the center of our decision making and look deep within ourselves for the answers to our questions. Through that process, we will receive the guidance we need to do what we have the power to do; and that will lead us directly into the niche in the kingdom only we can fill.

SEVEN

Speed Bumps and the Long Haul: Finding Balance over a Lifetime

 alancing our lives on our spiritual center is never a static but a dynamic endeavor. As we seek to make Jesus the center of our spiritual beings and use the framework of discipleship to order our lives, we face the ongoing challenge of making that framework fit the ever-changing circumstances in which we find ourselves.

The struggle isn't new. In the beginning the apostles found themselves preaching and teaching and bringing multitudes of people into relationship with Christ. Life and ministry proceeded smoothly. Then suddenly the circumstances changed. People began to feel uncomfortable with the way things were progressing. I've always appreciated the small glimpse of the early church's growing pains found in the Book of Acts because it reminds me that even the apostles had to do some major troubleshooting. While the following story relates to the growth of the church, I believe it also has some lessons for our interior lives.

> As the believers rapidly multiplied, there were rumblings of discontent. Those who spoke Greek complained against those who spoke Hebrew, saying that their widows were being discriminated against in the daily distribution of food. So the Twelve called a meeting of all the believers.

"We apostles should spend our time preaching and teaching the word of God, not administering a food program," they said. "Now look around among yourselves, brothers, and select seven men who are well respected and are full of the Holy Spirit and wisdom. We will put them in charge of this business. Then we can spend our time in prayer and preaching and teaching the word."

This idea pleased the whole group, and they chose the following: Stephen (a man full of faith and the Holy Spirit), Philip, Procorus, Nicanor, Timon, Parmenas, and Nicolas of Antioch (a Gentile convert to the Jewish faith, who had now become a Christian). These seven were presented to the apostles, who prayed for them as they laid their hands on them. (Acts 6:1-6, NLT)

Suddenly this group of new believers needed to reevaluate how it ministered. We experience a similar pattern. Things are going well. We feel comfortable with the way our responsibilities and commitments are unfolding. Then suddenly the particulars of our lives change and we have to reevaluate they way we are doing things. Just as the fledgling church needed to determine how to deal with a new set of circumstances while remaining focused on its mission, so we too must continually determine how to deal with changing circumstances while remaining focused on discipleship and centeredness.

Balance and centeredness occur over the entire expanse of our lifetimes. What works at one time in our lives may not be appropriate for other times. There may be times when discipleship requires that we give extra weight, for example, to parenting; at other times, to our jobs. We've seen how this is a healthy form of temporary fragmentation. Even as we strive to live balanced and centered lives right now, using our center as the reference point by which we make our everyday decisions, looking at the totality of our lives helps us sense the depth of the wholeness that God following creates.

The Art of Setting the Pace

A phrase from the story of Jacob and Esau helps me with this. After the brothers reunited and planned to journey together, Jacob said, "I will lead on slowly . . . . according to the pace of the children" (Gen. 33:14). Esau wanted to lead the way for the entire entourage, but Jacob knew that in his group were young animals and small children who could not travel at the ordinary pace. So he told Esau to go on ahead while he stayed behind with the children.

This simple line helps me realize that there will be times in my life when I must travel not at my own pace, but at the pace of someone else. For many of us our children will set that pace, for others, aging parents might set it. For others still, a job rather than another person may demand an appropriate speed. But no matter who or what the pace setter, if our center is Christ and we flex according to Christ's individual calls to us, we will experience the wholeness God intends for our lives. We will not feel we are losing anything by traveling more slowly or quickly than those around us.

My experience in deciding not to increase my workload in light of Nathan's school difficulties highlights this for me. At that time, God desired that I travel at Nathan's pace, not my own. I was still able to experience a sense of balance and wholeness because though Nathan initiated my decision, Christ remained my center and I was flexible to Christ's call at that season in my life. Recognizing that it is okay to sometimes favor varying elements of our lives helps us to view wholeness from the perspective of our entire lifetime. When we look over the long haul, we will see that each segment of life balanced out the other. The period I spent nurturing Nathan during his school struggles will balance out the period I spend in intensive ministry outside the home.

Connected to this recognition is the fact that balance does not necessarily mean an equality of parts. We do not experience wholeness by trying to experience everything to an equal degree, or by trying to experience exactly what everyone else is experiencing. Wholeness does not happen because we add one part work, one part play, one part relationships, and one part personal time. Wholeness doesn't result when we try to make another person's lifestyle our own. Christ-centeredness leads to a wholeness that is always more than the simple sum of our parts. We never gain it by following a generic formula whereby we add exact amounts of this and that and come up with wholeness. In reality, our wholeness may derive from a seemingly lopsided compilation.

For example, God may be calling some of us to a life without elements that are crucial to other persons' wholeness. My father had a friend, Brother Simon, who was a Trappist monk. God had called him to a life of celibacy and devotion to the religious life. While I never met Brother Simon, my father enjoyed a regular correspondence with him and shared some of those letters with me; I even received a few myself. In reading these letters, I immediately sensed the depth of Brother Simon's spirit. He followed Christ and received a wholeness and balance that sharply contrasted with the apparent austerity and limitations of his life. For Brother Simon, following with integrity meant giving up a part of life that the majority of us find very important. Because he was centered on Christ, he experienced a deep sense of wholeness.

Still, at certain points our lives may appear out of balance because we have a particular focus. Fortunately we can experience balance and wholeness even if others cannot perceive it. This is why it is not always helpful to compare ourselves to others. The things that contribute to another's balance and centeredness at this moment in time may not contribute to ours at the same moment. That is why one woman can experience balance and Christ-centeredness while staying home with her children, and another woman can have an equally strong sense of balance and Christ-centeredness while pursuing a career. What may seem like completely different commitments can actually produce the same result.

The strange but wonderful thing about balance and Christ-centeredness is that they look and feel different for each of us. The components of a balanced life for me may throw your life completely out of whack. John and I have a good friend whom we affectionately refer to as an "activity freak." He is always on the move. Requiring only about four hours of sleep a night, he can pack a great deal more into his days than I could ever pack into mine. Generally speaking, he thrives on activity. While his job demands that he travel quite a bit, he has still coached his children's soccer teams, served at his church, and volunteered in the community.

He is at his best when his life is very busy; he gets antsy in a lull.

In contrast, I need eight hours of sleep a night, although I can occasionally make it on less. I need downtime to regroup and begin to feel stressed if too much is happening in my life, especially for long periods of time. That stress usually surfaces at 3:00 A.M. when I wake up in a cold sweat, listing all the things I need to accomplish. When I compare myself to my friend, as unfortunately I sometimes do, I always feel lazy. The truth, however, is that I am not lazy, and my life would be a disaster and completely out of balance if I tried to duplicate his.

So while we strive for balance and Christ-centeredness in each moment of our lives, we will recognize the wholeness God gives only over an entire lifetime. When we look back over our lives, we will see how at one time we gave more energy to child rearing, while at another we devoted energy to volunteer work, and our lives still reflected wholeness and balance.

Decision Making with the Future in Mind

In addition, what makes for a balanced and centered life is not necessarily the actual decisions that we make, because there are many things that we might choose and still gain a sense of balance. The key to balance and centeredness is the process that leads to the decision. The commitments we make must be in tune not only with what is "good enough" for us in a particular moment, they must also be conducive to the balance and centeredness we seek over the course of our entire lives.

We touched on this in our contrast between roles and relationships. We can view motherhood, for example, as a role, and make our decisions based on our performance of that role in the present moment or circumstance. If we do that, however, we run the substantial risk that over the course of time, our decisions will have less and less to do with us (or our children) and more and more to do with our perceived role of mother. Then when our children are grown and independent, we will have little left for ourselves.

If, on the other hand, we view motherhood as the relationship between mother and child, we will make our decisions with both sides of the relationship in mind. We will value the needs of our children, but we will also value our own needs. In this way, we are assured over the course of a lifetime that while the relationship may change, it will not disappear, and both mother and child will be able to grow in ways that lead to balance and centeredness.

I have experienced this need to attend to both the long and the short run in several of my work-related decisions, the incident with Nathan again providing the easiest example. While I chose not to increase my workload, I did not choose to give up my work completely. Giving up my work certainly was an option, and God could have led me that way. But giving up ministry completely was not conducive to the wholeness of my overall life, which included my future beyond my children.

Full Discipleship and Balance

However we choose to utilize our gifts in following Christ, we cannot escape the extreme nature of Christ's call upon our lives. This is the most difficult part of the journey toward balance and centeredness to understand. For even as we have talked about discipleship as the framework for centeredness, even as we have explored balance as a lifelong endeavor, we cannot miss the fact that Jesus' call to us does not look very balanced. Remember the Lord's words to the rich man, who had kept all the commandments: "There is still one thing lacking. Sell all that you own and distribute the money to the poor, and you will have treasure in heaven; then come, follow me" (Luke 18:22). Or Jesus' response to Peter and the rest of the disciples when they refused to comprehend the suffering Jesus was about to endure: "If any of you wants to be my follower, . . . you must put aside your selfish ambition, shoulder your cross, and follow me. If you try to keep your life for yourself, you will lose it. But if you give up your life for my sake and for the sake of the Good News, you will find true life" (Mark 8:34-35, NLT). Or Jesus' instruction when he discovered that the disciples had all been arguing about which one was the greatest: "Whoever wants to be first must be last of all and servant of all" (Mark 9:35).

Jesus did not tell people to follow when it fit into their schedule, or when they were in the "right place" spiritually. Jesus simply said, "Follow me" with the implicit addition of now—do it now. When Jesus called people, he never asked them to place their commitment to him on an even par with their commitments to the other things in their lives. It had to be the top priority. Jesus made clear that if you were going to respond to his call, you had to be willing to lose your life for his sake. And people did. They dropped what they were doing and followed. They gave up their lives for Jesus' sake.

What are we to do with the extreme nature of this claim on our lives? How can that possibly gel with any semblance of balance? At the heart of it all is focus. While Jesus always challenged people to move out of their comfort zones in order to deepen their relationship with God, Jesus never called anyone to do anything he or she could not do. His call may have been stringent, but it was not impossible—especially with God's help. The rich man could have followed, he simply chose not to because his focus was on his money rather than on his relationship with God. When the disciples followed Jesus, their world may have turned upside down, but they still had to eat and sleep and attend to all the other activities of daily living. The difference was that their focus had completely changed. Even Paul, who gave himself so completely to Jesus, continued to make tents and work to earn a living (Acts 18:3; 1 Thess. 2:9).

There will always be tension between the extreme nature of Christ's call to follow and our response to that call. Well there should be. If we try to smooth out the differences too completely, we risk self-deception, a sense of following when we are not following at all. At the same time, we should not use the radical nature of Christ's call as an excuse not to follow—"I can't do that now, look at all my responsibilities!" Christ's call to follow may be extreme, but it comes to each of us in the context of our own lives; Christ calls us to respond *within* those contexts. It is the focus of our life that must change, even if the constraints that surround us do not.

The Spoke of Flexibility

When suddenly confronted with changed circumstances and the need for reevaluation, as the early church was, we would do well to learn from the apostles' example. Flexibility proved to be a winning strategy for the church. Because everyone agreed that the current balance of responsibility needed adjustment and the believers were willing to make the necessary changes to accommodate new challenges, they were able to adapt a new, workable model for fulfilling their mission. So we too, using the spoke of flexibility, can adapt as our needs and those of the people around us change.

It is only as we flex that we embrace the wholeness that Christ-centeredness brings. Recognizing that the only consistent element of our lives is Christ's call, we understand that the ways we express our discipleship will vary with the assignment Christ gives us at each stage. Again, we must realize that we can't see how the pieces fit from our short-sighted view. It is over the long haul that the scene will make sense. Following Christ through the surprising seasons of our lives will require trust; achieving a sense of wholeness will require flexibility.

Our journey toward balance and centeredness is a lifelong journey. While we may join others as we travel, and while fellow travelers may provide valuable support, our journey will belong to us and will be unlike any other person's. We will encounter obstacles, both from within ourselves and from the outside world. We will face forces that hinder our growth and seek to mold us into images that do not fit. But if we work to discover who we are, if we desire to come into relationship with God with our authentic selves, we can then find and live from Christ, our center.

Having found that center, we can place our relationship with God there—at the center of ourselves—and use that relationship as the guiding force in our lives. When we respond to Christ's dramatic call, discipleship becomes the framework on which we base our lives, and it informs the spokes of the wheel leading from our center to the outer regions of our lives. With that type of framework, regardless of how fast the merry-go-round may be spinning, no matter how much the forces of life may threaten to fling us out and off, we can stand firm; we can move toward our center for stability and strength, and we can experience the wholeness and integrity that God intended for our lives.

Questions for Reflection and Discussion

include these questions to enhance individual reflection and inspire personal action; however, you may adapt them for use with a small group. Our spiritual journey is not meant to be an isolated experience, but one that we share with fellow travelers. Particularly as we strive for a sense of balance in the face of all the competing demands of life, to share our experiences, both the victories and the challenges, can be immensely helpful. The connections we create and the bonds we forge often form the foundation of support and encouragement we need to continue on our journey with strength and perseverance.

INTRODUCTION: THE CALL TO BALANCE AND CENTEREDNESS

- Have you ever experienced your life to be like a ride on a whirling merry-go-round? If so, reflect on how you cope with the hectic pace of your life. What commitments demand your attention? Do you feel as though these commitments are in competition for your attention?

- During the next week, be aware of the ways your commitments might be in competition with one another. How are you responding to that competition?

- Reflect on the path that you have taken to arrive at the point where you now stand. Has your path been direct or indirect? If it was direct, spend a few moments thinking about what influenced you to make the choices you made as your life unfolded. List those influencers. If it was an indirect path, reflect on the issues that competed for your loyalty and attention. List those competing elements and what influenced you make the choices you made. Think about which influencers helped you most and how you can call on them in making future decisions.

- Where do you turn when you need to regain a sense of balance? To your own strategies? To God?

- List the spokes that have made up your "wheel" so far. Are they working to ensure a smooth ride? Why or why not?

- Over the next few weeks, be aware of the issues or demands that threaten your sense of balance. Identify their sources, and determine a healthy response to them.

- How has Christ fit into your spiritual journey thus far? Have you looked to Christ as a centering force in your life? Why or why not?

CHAPTER 1: THE BONDAGE OF STEREOTYPES:
SUSIE HOMEMAKER AND SUPERWOMAN

- What do you feel are the qualities of a "really good" woman? Why do you believe these qualities are so important?

- Reflect on whether and how society's Susie Homemaker ideal has limited your personal growth.

- During this week, be aware of the ways that society's Susie Homemaker ideal lingers in our collective consciousness. Identify instances where you or other women are struggling to meet that ideal. Be aware of the ways that ideal affects men's expectations as well.

- What kind of experiences have you had with the Superwoman ideal? How have you handled the competing demands?

- Look at your calendar of activities and commitments for the next several weeks. Are you being urged to take on more than is appropriate? What is the source of the demand? How are you responding? As you go about your activities, be alert to ways in which you are being pressured to be Superwoman.

- Have you ever experienced a disparity between what you feel God is calling you to do and what the church is encouraging you to do? Spend some time thinking about how you could resolve such a dilemma.

- What are some of the valuable elements of each of the myths we've discussed?

- Reflect on your feelings about Orpah. Was your opinion positive or negative? Have you ever experienced circumstances in which you felt that of two opposing choices, only one of them was right? Reflect on that experience.

- Make a list of the various commitments you have made recently. How has your faith entered into your decision-making process? How will these commitments affect your faith walk? Reflect on whether each commitment on your list hinders or energizes your faith development. Decide how you can remove yourself from those commitments that negatively affect you. Begin to do so.

- Reflect on the ways that pursuing excellence can sabotage you as you seek balance and wholeness.

- Complete the following sentences: "I can be a good enough [mother, wife, employee, etc.] as long as I _____." "I do not have to do _____ in order to be a good enough [mother, wife, employee, etc.]."

- Keep the concept of "good enough" in the back of your mind as you go through this next week. When you face choices, remind yourself of this concept as you work through your decision.

- Have you ever had the experience of being fragmented? If so, how did it affect you?

- Reflect on a time when it was necessary for you to attend more intently to one part of your life. Was this a transitory circumstance or did this become a pattern for you? If it was more than a phase, how has that affected your overall sense of wholeness?

- Spend some time thinking about the tendency of many women to become overextended—pulled apart by the many competing demands of their lives. Look at your calendar of commitments for the last several weeks and several upcoming ones. Is becoming overextended a standard operating procedure in your life? If so, what might you do to change it? Today, begin doing what is necessary to change this situation.

- If you have identified the sense of being pulled apart by many competing demands, reflect on how that has affected your sense of balance. How has it affected those around you?

- How have you experienced the different "selves" that make up your whole self? Are they able to talk to each other? Why or why not?

- As you implement your plan to alleviate your sense of fragmentation, be on guard for future commitments that would overextend you. During the weeks ahead, when you encounter such circumstances, remind yourself of the concept of temperance as a guideline in making your decisions.

CHAPTER 3: WHO AM I TODAY?: THE TYRANNY OF ROLES

- Reflect on the ways that roles have pigeonholed you during the various stages of your life.

- How have the blocks of trusting others more than yourself and focusing on your appearance hindered you from developing a genuine sense of yourself as a particular, authentic person created by God?

- Spend a moment focusing on the fear that if we are truly known we will not be loved. How has that fear affected your process of understanding who you are?

- Have you experienced a preoccupation with roles that has hindered a relationship? Reflect on that experience. What might you do to reestablish the relationship as primary? Do it today.

- During the next week, be aware of the various roles you have accepted. What is your focus? Is it the role, or the relationship that grounds the role? How might you be deliberate about emphasizing the relationships that are the foundation for the roles of your life? Do it as the opportunity arises.

CHAPTER 4: THE SEARCH FOR OUR CENTER:
DISCOVERING WHO WE ARE

- Spend a few moments in silent meditation, opening yourself to experiencing Jesus as the "particular" that makes the "abstract" God real for you. Be aware of the Spirit of Christ who lives not only in the past, but also in the present.

- How have you named yourself before God in the past? Name yourself before God as you are in this moment.

- Write your own psalm through which to approach God with your authentic self. If you wish, use a psalm from Scripture as a guide for wording your own emotions, observations, and desires.

- Allow God to rename you in this moment as God sees you: unique and loved from the start.

CHAPTER 5: DISCIPLESHIP AND CENTEREDNESS:
FOLLOWING JESUS' CALL

- What are some of the messages you are hearing as you attempt to follow Christ? Are you sure they are coming from Christ?

- During the coming weeks, be aware of the various messages you are hearing about your discipleship. Make deliberate efforts to discern whether those messages are truly from Christ.

- Enlist the support of family or close friends for spiritual guidance as you try to discern God's voice. Others are often able to perceive gifts and opportunities of which we are unaware. They can also provide invaluable confirmation or caution. As you undertake this process, though, remember that God's call to you is your own; others may or may not hear it. If you hear it, it is yours.

- How would listening to Jesus' word to Martha push you out of your comfort zone?

- If you took responsibility for your own discipleship, what would have to change in your life? Make the necessary changes to assume greater responsibility for your discipleship. Find others who can encourage you and hold you accountable in these changes.

- Are there idols in your life? Reflect on the possibility that some of the things you have considered virtuous may actually be idolatrous. Begin praying that God would free you from your connection to idols and dedicate yourself to turning away from them.

- How do you feel about Jesus' strong words that place discipleship above family?

- Reflect on your feelings about your time. Do you value it? How do you spend it? What demands most of it? Why? Based on your reflections, create a strategy that maximizes your good use of it. Begin implementing your strategy today.

- How do you see yourself contributing to "the common good"?

- Look at your calendar for the next few days and intentionally schedule a time for personal reflection regarding your calling. During this time, dedicate yourself to making the necessary changes to confidently assert that your time is important, your life is important, and both have value even when you are not actively working to serve or please others.

CHAPTER 6: TO FIND OUR NICHE:
ASKING THE RIGHT QUESTIONS

- Think about the strategy of asking "Why?" before asking "What?" when deciding on a course of action. How does it relate to taking responsibility for your own discipleship? How would this strategy help you in moving toward a more balanced and centered life?

- During the next week, as you encounter decisions, deliberately ask yourself "Why?" before moving to "What?"

- Spend some time assessing your gifts and talents. Write them all down. Begin by focusing on the things you enjoy, recalling that joy may actually be the Spirit working to guide you. Meditate on your abilities and open yourself to the possibility that God is calling you to use one or more of them for God's purpose.

- As you meditate on your abilities, focus on one in particular. How might you use this gift for God? Do it today.

- If you applied the concept "Do what you have the power to do today" to your life, what things might you begin doing? How might that give you confidence and boldness?

- Do what you have the power to do today.

CHAPTER 7: SPEED BUMPS AND THE LONG HAUL: FINDING
BALANCE OVER A LIFETIME

- How is the need for reevaluation apparent in your life?

- Schedule on your calendar periodic occasions for evaluation and reevaluation. Remember that circumstances may dictate your rethinking things at times other than those you have scheduled. Be open to that need, but determine to take the necessary time.

- Ponder the idea that balance is something that occurs over the course of a lifetime. Are you currently traveling at someone else's pace? If so, how might the recognition of balance occurring over the course of a lifetime enhance your experience? What might you do differently as a result of gaining that recognition?

- If you are traveling at someone else's pace, identify things you might be able to do to attend to your own calling while still maintaining your commitment to the other. Find ways to implement them.

- Reflect on the concept that the actual decisions we make are not what produce a balanced and centered life; the process that leads to those decisions is. How might this concept alter or strengthen your commitments?

Notes

INTRODUCTION

1. Maxie Dunnam and Kimberly Dunnam Reisman, *The Workbook on Virtues and the Fruit of the Spirit* (Nashville, Tenn.: Upper Room Books™, 1998), 71.

CHAPTER 1

1. Mary Ellen Ashcroft, *Balancing Act: How Women Can Lose Their Roles and Find Their Callings* (Downers Grove, Ill.: InterVarsity Press, 1996), 46-47.

2. Walter Houghton, *The Victorian Frame of Mind 1830-1870* (New Haven, Conn.: Yale University Press, 1957), 54-89.

3. Stephanie Coontz, *The Way We Never Were: American Families and the Nostalgic Trap* (New York: Basic Books, 1992), 156.

4. *The Choice Works of John Ruskin* (New York: The F. M. Lupton Publishing Company, 1900), 78.

5. Ibid., 79.

6. Betty Friedan, *The Feminine Mystique* (New York: Bantam Doubleday Dell Publishing Group, Inc., 1983), 34-35.

7. Ibid., 33, 31.

8. Ibid., 71-72.

9. Annie Roiphe, *Fruitful: Living the Contradictions: A Memoir of Modern Motherhood* (New York: Penguin Books, 1996), 8.

10. Ibid., 29.

11. Karen S. Schneider et al., "Ryan's Express," *People Weekly*, 21 December 1998, 106.

CHAPTER 2

1. Tedd Arnold, *Parts* (New York: Scholastic, Inc., 1997), 16.

2. Michele Gaither Sparks, "Robes and Rattles," *The Asbury Herald* 108 (1997), 14.

3. Maxie Dunnam, *Dancing At My Funeral* (Atlanta: Forum House Publishers, 1973), 61-62.

4. Leontyne Price cited in Maxie Dunnam, *Barefoot Days of the Soul* (Waco, Texas: Word, Inc., 1975), 61.

CHAPTER 3

1. Ashcroft, *Balancing Act: How Women Can Lose Their Roles and Find Their Callings*, 96.

2. Dr. Bernadine Healy, "A Medical Revolution," *Newsweek* Special Edition, Spring/Summer 1999, 64.

CHAPTER 4

1. Helen Keller, *Teacher* (Garden City, N.Y.: Doubleday & Company, Inc., 1955), 8.

2. Ibid., 40.

CHAPTER 5

1. Dorothy L. Sayers, "Unpopular Opinions: Twenty-One Essays" in *A Matter of Eternity: Selections from the Writings of Dorothy L. Sayers* (Grand Rapids: William B. Eerdmans Publishing Company, 1973), 95-96.

2. Ashcroft, *Balancing Act: How Women Can Lose Their Roles and Find Their Callings*, 173.

3. Ibid.

4. Dorothy Sayers, "Are Women Human?" in *A Matter of Eternity: Selections from the Writings of Dorothy L. Sayers*, 26.

CHAPTER 6

1. Helen Bruch Pearson, *Do What You Have the Power to Do: Studies of Six New Testament Women* (Nashville, Tenn.: Upper Room Books™, 1992), 12.

2. Ibid., 46-47.